Love will Overcome

Talks and writings of Henri Boulad, compiled by Kenneth Payne

An environmentally friendly book printed and bound in England by www.printondemand-worldwide.com

Mixed Sources
Product group from well-managed forests, and other controlled sources
www.fsc.org Cert no. TT-COC-002641
© 1996 Forest Stewardship Council
FSC

PEFC Certified
This product is from sustainably managed forests and controlled sources
www.pefc.org
PEFC
PEFC/16-33-415

This book is made entirely of chain-of-custody materials

FastPrint Publishing
www.fast-print.net/store.php

LOVE WILL OVERCOME

A catalogue record for this book is available from the British Library

ISBN 978-178035-748-5

First published 2014 by
FASTPRINT PUBLISHING
Peterborough, England.

Contents

Introduction
By Kenneth Payne

Henri Boulad, Born in Alexandria in 1931, personifies what this city used to represent: a melting pot of universality. His origins are Syrian and Italian, his nationality Egyptian and Lebanese, his rite Greco-Byzantine, and his cultural background French. A disciple of Pascal, Teilhard de Chardin and Simone Weil, he is endowed with an oriental soul and an occidental mind, and dreams of reconciling and uniting the most varying spheres such as: philosophy and theology, physics and mystics, sexuality and chastity, action and contemplation, sociology and religion, economics, politics and faith. And thus his situation is in direct descent from that "Christian humanism" which characterises Jesuit spirituality and that of its founder Ignatius of Loyola. With his capacity for opening up new realms, he is also at the vanguard of post-modernism, determined by its interdisciplinarity.

His studies of spirituality, literature, philosophy, theology and psychology, led him from Lebanon to France and the USA, where he obtained a master's degree in psychology in the University of Chicago. As teacher, spiritual guide, lecturer, teacher of theology, he was successively entrusted with the function of superior of the Jesuit community in Alexandria and of regional superior of the Jesuits of Egypt. He was for many years the director of Caritas-Egypt and vice-president of Caritas-Internationalis for the Middle East and North Africa. In acknowledgement of his efforts in the service of the most destitute, he was nominated Officier and then Commandeur of the Ordre national du Mérite by the French government.

A man of ceaseless searching, he finds he never arrives at a conclusion. His claims for solidarity and reconciliation between faith and reason, tradition and modernity urge him to query and question everything continuously. Enamoured of risk, fond of paradox, gladly provoking, Henri Boulad is a personality who cannot be classified because he does not fit into any category.

He has published numerous books in a dozen languages, but, so far, his only book in English, at Crossroad, New York and SCM Press, London, is out of print: *All is Grace*. Published in 1991, this is a challenging spiritual work on God, man and the mystery of time. However, some of his talks, interviews and articles have been collected together and made available, typewritten on A4 leaflets. What follows are extracts from these and they form an "aperitif", an appetiser and incentive to read further and hopefully see more of his works published in the English language.

My thanks extends, first of all, to my good friend, Marcel Peterhans from Switzerland, who, through his enthusiasm subsequent to hearing and meeting Henri Boulad, introduced me to some of his writings. I then made contact with Hidda Westenberger in Austria, the authorised editor for all international publications of Fr Boulad. She also worked so hard to translate into German Father Boulad's talks and writings for 14 books, all published in Austria, and she encouraged me to work for his recognition in the English speaking world. I hope, therefore, that this somewhat inadequate presentation of some of Henri Boulad's thoughts and ideas will help to bring about his recognition.

On one occasion Fr Boulad claims that he is trying to bring nearer to people a certain truth which seems otherwise too far-reaching. His way of teaching is always to stir up and shake his audience, stating thoughts in an extreme way in order to challenge and make people think and react. This after all, was the method of the Jewish Rabbi, and of Jesus.

I have grouped the extracts in a very general way according to subject matter, giving the origin of the passage, the key to which is listed below:

A "Resurrection or Reincarnation? No one can come to the Father except through me."

Discussion group in Austria, June 1993

B "Resurrection or Reincarnation? Vatican II and Christian Fundamentalism."

C "New wine into New Skins for the Church of Tomorrow" – Conference in Austria, April 1996

D "The Thousand Faces of the Spirit" – Conference to students, teachers and guests in Graz, Austria, 1997

E "The Creative Energy of Suffering" – Conference in Alexandria, 1979

F "The Spirituality of Risk" – Conference in Klagenfurt, Austria, 1993

G. "The Thousand Faces of the Spirit" – Lecture in Klagenfurt, Austria, 1992

H "Mystical Prayer: Three Zones of the Human Personality" – Conference in Alexandria, 1975

I "The Mystics of Teilhard de Chardin" – Conference at Pécs (Hungary) 1997

J "Learning to Become, Man has to invest himself" in Pécs (Hungary) 1997

K "The Courage to be" – Conference in Budapest, 1997

L New Parables 1994: "The Pool", "The Bicycle", "The Illegal Immigrant" translated by Christa Pongratz-Lippit

M "Sapentia – the Taste of God in our Lives" – Conference in Prague 1998

N "The mystical Path" – Encounter in Prague 1998

O "The Secret Energy in Us" – Conference in Prague, 1998

P "Divine Freedom and Human Freedom" – Alexandria, 1979

Q "The Endless Horizon: the Future of our Religions" – Conference in Klagenfurt (Austria), 1999

R "Beauty, Aesthetics, Enjoyment or Mystical Experience?" – Conference at Wolfsberg Castle, Austria, 2001

S "God has a Heart and it Suffers" – Conference at Linz in Austria, 1999

T "Mysticism and Politics" – Conference in Villach, Austria, 1999

U "The Fear of Freedom" Chapter 3 of "Determine Your Life in Freedom" – Jesuit Periodical, Munich 2000

V Interview between Henri Boulad S.J. and Mag. Johannes Kaup "Love and Immortality", given in English at the ORF Radio Studio in Vienna (Austria) 16 July 2007

W Letter to Pope Benedict XVI, 18 July 2007

X "Amour-Oralité – Eucharistie" being 7 conferences in Geneva, October 2001

Y Translated from the French by Louis Bardou

Chapter 1:
God and the Trinity – Why?

I want to get away from a certain concept of God which has become part of our flesh and blood, and which is very difficult for us to get rid of. We have inherited this concept of God from Greek philosophy, God as a super power, and his greatness is beyond all imagination. In the Old Testament we also have a kind of omnipotence which is perpetuated in a certain sense through our liturgy and in our prayer books. When we start our prayers with the words "Almighty God", or we end our prayers with the sentence: "For yours is the kingdom, the power and the glory for ever and ever". We get an idea of God who is a kind of super king enthroned in the heavens above.

At other times we say that God is perfectly happy and enjoying being in heaven because it would be a kind of humiliation for him not to be at that level, he has to keep his position as God, otherwise he would not be God. In a vision such as that of Isaiah who saw God enthroned in heaven, surrounded by angels, archangels, cherubim, and seraphim all glorifying, adoring and praising him – we have a picture of God enjoying celestial life, and being honoured. All these representations of God are inherited from a medieval, oriental or ancient vision of kings and emperors which suited a certain mentality, and this concept of God has generated in people a certain attitude of submission, of adoration and of fear which is still haunting them. Additionally, religion has fostered in us this attitude which we find difficult to overcome. The main quality or the main virtue which is asked of the believer is fear, fear. You have to fear God. The concept of adoration is linked to a slavish attitude in the presence of God.

The New Testament wanted to change this attitude but I don't think that people have done so yet. When Jesus said: "I don't call you servants but friends", it did not change much in the attitude of today's believer. We still call human beings servants of God in our Christian Latin liturgy, and it is even worse in Arabic: "Abd" means slave. It's horrible! And the plural "abid", means human being. So human beings have been called slaves until now. What is worth stressing is that this concept of an all-powerful God has generated an all-powerful Man. This means that when you have before you a concept of a God who takes revenge, who is aggressive and punishes people, then you develop a kind of model. This model of a certain type of God has shaped the model of a certain type of Man.

Man's history so far has been a long succession of wars and battles, killings and massacres. This kind of God produces this kind of Man. I would call this relationship what Hegel has defined as a master/slave relationship – the dialectic of master and slaves. If you are strong you dominate, if you are weak you have to bow down, lean on, accept and obey. A man like Blaise Pascal made a sudden conversion in that famous night when he finally discovered the true God of revelation. He called it a night of fire. For one hour and a half he had a fantastic experience of the true God and he wrote down: "God of Abraham, God of Isaac, God of Jacob, not the God of scientist and philosopher but the God of Jesus Christ." And from that moment on, Pascal, the great philosopher and scientist, suddenly became the servant of the poor, helping the destitute and giving his home and his life to them. This is the core of Christian revelation – the God who descends from heaven above in order to be close to Man.

(Ref S)

I will try and tell a story of God, or place the concept of God in the frame of a legend: "Once upon a time there was God, sitting on a big chair, and being happy to be God. And God Almighty said; "I am the Being, I am everything, I am all-powerful. I am what I am, God". After a while he looked at his watch and said: "It is quite boring being God, and especially being God for the whole of eternity." So, all of a sudden, God felt within himself a kind of whisper, a suggestion telling him to move forward to move outward, telling him: "Try to love! Try to live!" And this whisper was so powerful, so intense within God, that all of a sudden, God – "pfsst ....!" - exploded. This was the real beginning of God. Now you will ask me: "And before that, was God not God?" No, he was not! God started when life started in him, and when love was born within.

So, if we tell a story as I did, all of a sudden you can see how God was – because otherwise he would not have been God. Therefore, from the very beginning, the beginning of the beginning, God is in a state of explosion, in a state of expansion, in a state of life, in a state of love.

(Ref D)

Sometimes we say: God is three in one and one in three. Why? This is the Father, the Son, the Holy Spirit. So, if I ask you where the Father is, you will say: "Here!" "Where is the Son?" you will say: "There!" "Where is the Spirit?" You will say: "There!" Wrong! This is not the Spirit. The Spirit is neither here, nor there, nor anywhere.

The Spirit is a dynamic force moving from one to the other. He is nowhere, because he is everywhere. This dynamic force prompts the two to give each other to one another, and it brings them together at the end of the movement. So imagine that you push three circles within each other, then you have a reconstruction of God as with a puzzle. The Father is there (the Source) and the Son is there. And where is the Spirit? The Spirit is inside, flowing, bursting, sparkling, exploding, living, loving. Without the Spirit we cannot understand God. Without the Spirit, God remains a monolithic and static block.

I live in Egypt which is an Islamic country. And the Moslems cannot understand why we try to do gymnastics with God. It was so simple to say that God is God for ever and ever. It seems more logical, it seems more philosophical, it seems more natural, it seems evident that God is that way. And, most Christians don't understand why we try to complicate things; if we can simplify them. Just ask any Christian why we have a Trinitarian God. He will say: "Ask a priest about it!" 99% of Christian's don't know why God is Trinitarian, or why he is not just ONE. The answer is: because we believe in a living God, in a loving God. And I cannot imagine another God. Not because I am a Christian, not because the Church has said that there is the Father, the Son and the Holy Spirit, but because to me this is the only logical existence of God.

(Ref D)

Why is God not one and alone? Why is there a Trinity? Why is the Greek God, the philosophical God, the Moslem God not our God? Is there any reason why God is Trinity? And is there any logic in this mystery of Trinity? And what is the role of the Spirit in this fundamental, original mystery of our faith?

I would say that the Spirit is that which makes God God. Without the Spirit, there is no God. Why? Because we call God "the Being", "the one who is" and this is how he revealed himself to Moses in the Book of Exodus. "I am what I am", "I am the one who is", Jahweh – the one who is. To be – for God – is to lose whatever he has in order to be, to become. God becomes God in as far as he loses himself, he loses his divinity. It's in losing himself that God becomes God. Of course, when we say that he becomes God this is completely heretical. God cannot become God – he is God from eternity to eternity. But to use human language and to express myself in a better way, I would put this essence of God in a frame of time, in a chronological succession of instances in order to make it clear, but at the end of what I am going to say, we have to suppress what is inherited or historical just to put it in one, eternal instant.

It is in springing out of himself, it is in losing himself, it is in dispossessing himself that God is. The being is realizing itself in as far as the having is lost. When God has his divinity, possesses his divinity, he is not God. God has to lose what he has in order to be what he is. And this springing force, this pushing energy within God, letting him empty himself from himself is what we call the Spirit. The Spirit is this inner force within the divinity which makes God live in a state of extasis (ex-stasis = to stay out of oneself). God is by his essence an ex-stasis; otherwise he would not be God. And it is because God is extasis that he is Trinity, otherwise he would not be Trinity. He would be the Moslem or the Greek God of the philosophers.

The extasis of God, out of himself, is the begetting of the Son. The Son is the result of God emptying himself. When he empties himself, he generates what we call the Son. The Son receives for himself the whole being of God, and in a certain sense God becomes Father. Before begetting the Son, God is not Father. He is simply nobody. In begetting the Son, he gives all – all that he has – to the Son and this is the extasis of God. And the Son receives the totality of divinity.

(Ref G)

Chapter 2: Creation and Incarnation

The first to have a spirituality of risk is God. God is the first to practise risk. God likes risk, and the first risk was to create a world, a universe. Creation is in itself the greatest risk which God has ever taken. We can hardly imagine what it represents, creation as a big adventure, a fantastic adventure which God has decided to embark on, because creation was unpredictable at the beginning in a certain sense. The way that scientists describe or explain the beginning of the universe, the big bang, is just a kind of boiling matter without shape, without form, without any visible aim, what the bible calls "tohu wa bohu", seemed to go in a haphazard way throughout space and in this matter, as we now know through science, there was no mechanical movement planned beforehand. But we know through the *Uncertainty of Relation* by Werner Heisenberg that even matter itself has a certain degree of spontaneity. Even matter is unpredictable; there is a kind of mini-freedom which gives matter a kind of spontaneity to develop in ways which are not planned beforehand. So we can see the universe left partly to itself to develop in its own way, and at the same time God having a plan for the end but willing to give the universe a self-deciding process from which it could develop itself from itself.

And evolution has invented itself by itself through a self-creating process with so many unpredictable crossroads. At each crossroad God seems to be trying to put evolution on the right track but at the same time he wants to respect this spontaneity of things because creation is giving to beings the dignity of being their own decision-makers. This is creation. Creation is not a pattern imposed by God where everything is decided, creation could have evolved in a different way, in so many other ways, but there is a self-deciding process within creation which makes it responsible for itself. Of course, it's not freedom in the human sense but spontaneity. I would say: evolution is the triumph of the improbable. At the pinnacle of everything you have human freedom.

What makes things difficult is that if you move just one element of the whole universe in the wrong way, the whole complex of the universe has to be reshaped. And we know now from physics, that in moving this glass here the furthest star feels it because any movement in any part of the universe involves the whole universe. Any choice I make for myself, in my life, has repercussions in the whole cosmos and this is why any wrong choice I make in my life means that the whole system has to be recreated and this is what I call Redemption. Redemption is a continuous rebuilding, restructuring, reinventing the whole of creation.

(Ref F)

Some people even believe that God worked for only six days in order to create the universe, on the Seventh Day, the Sabbath, he stopped and had a rest. No! My interpretation, along with that of other theologians, is that the Seventh Day of creation has not yet taken place; it is not behind us but ahead of us. This day will come at the end of history. Do you believe that the creation of Man happened once and for all? No, Man is being created; we are on the move because the act of creation is not yet completed. Maybe we are just at the beginning? Sometimes I feel we are still living in 'prehistoric times'. It is not God alone who is creating Man, but Man together with God; both are sitting on the river bank, moulding the human being of tomorrow, this future Man, fully responsible for himself, for others, and for the world. History is the expression of this joint creation.

(Ref T)

From the very beginning God immerses himself in matter. The spirit of God existed from the very beginning, in this Big Bang which, as science reveals to us, is the starting point of the universe. In this primeval Tohu wa bohu, in this plasma (but it was not yet plasma, plasma is a state of matter in development) this initial matter is totally impregnated with the spirit of God from the very beginning. The spirit of God is not something from outside but from inside. God did not shape the world with two hands like mine, he shaped the world from inside and made it evolve into higher and higher states of being.

How much deeper is this vision! Not an exterior God created the world but an ulterior God, shaping and pushing and animating it. A kind of God who is the soul of the world, or as Teilhard de Chardin puts it: the spirit of the earth, 1'Esprit de la Terre. This spirit is at work, not *doing* things but allowing things to get done by themselves. Oh, what a beautiful thought! God does not create the world; God lets the world create itself by itself. That is self-creation. A fascinating vision! God gives the world the power to create itself, the dignity, the joy of being a self-creating process.

How does this process take place? Through love, love, love! Love is the most fundamental force, the most fundamental energy of the cosmos, even at the level of atoms. What brings a neutron together with an electron? This marriage is the first embrace in the cosmos. When a proton embraces an electron, it is like a boy embracing a girl. Exactly the same. This attraction between positive and negative poles of matter is in its most initial phase a force which will later on become love, but at this stage it is attraction. This attraction pushes each element towards another element in order to build up a new unity. The unity of atoms, molecules, mega-molecules is the result of a current of energy which is basically an initial form of love called the law of the universe. At the level of mankind, we cannot yet call it love, it is, the ancestor of love.

By this process, what was hidden deep down starts to appear? I would say that evolution is the unfolding of a reality which existed in primitive matter from the very beginning. What does *unfolding* mean? It means showing up, letting what is inside come to the surface. Everything is in matter from the very beginning of evolution, for 13 billion years. In this very primitive nucleus of the world *you* and *I* are present, with our faces, our organisms! Imagine the whole of humanity, of mankind, present from the very beginning, in a different, a very primitive way, not yet unfolded as a self but already present, from the beginning of evolution as a promise, as a dream. Do you know the story of Martin Luther King? He once sang: "I have a dream!" This dream has come true! If you ask the primitive matter before life appeared: "How about you, matter?" matter will answer, "I have a dream." "What is your dream?" "To become a wonderful baby, a face, a human being!" Deep down in primitive matter there is a dream, and this dream is man!

Scientists have recently discovered the entropic principle. What does it mean? It means that the whole of evolution is orientated towards a goal, towards a "telos" as they say in Greek, a telos which means an aim, a goal, an objective. The theory of evolution presents evolution as a kind of gambling process, a haphazard process, a trial by error process, along which man finally appeared quite by chance! How? Why? Nobody knows! There were 1 million chances for man not to appear, but he did because he was hidden inside matter and he directed the evolutionary process in such a way that he had to appear, because he was planned from the very beginning. This is what we call the entropic principle.

Man becomes the key to the universe and to evolution. If you want to understand the whole process, don't try to see it from below, look at it from above. Man is the last arrival in evolution, but the one who comes at the end is the one who was there at the beginning. If you want to understand the whole process, try to see where it goes. Which direction does it tend to go? Looking at the end, at the result, you will understand. This is why Teilhard de Chardin's whole vision is anthropocentric. Man is the key.

Nowadays we speak a lot about ecology. Ecology is all about nature, trees, animals! Fantastic! It reminds me of St. Francis of Assisi and his deep relationship with nature, animals, plants, the sun, the moon, the stars ... with the whole cosmos. This harmony which St. Francis discovered is exactly the same as the one discovered by Teilhard de Chardin. This mystical vision of the world is not only poetical for Teilhard, it is also scientific. He shows the link and the deep connection, the relationship between myself and the cat, the tree, the moon, the sun. They all are my brothers and sisters. Because we were one in the past, and I am their explanation, I am the dream hidden within the tree, I am the dream hidden within the animal, the sea, the flowers, the sun. I am the answer. If you go deep down into the tree, you will find its dream "I have a dream!" "What is your dream, good tree?" "I dream of becoming man!" "And you, my dear dog?" "I dream of becoming man!" Each reality of the cosmos has deep down within itself a dream, and this dream is you, is me!

Is man really the end of evolution? Are you and I really at the end of a process? No! Teilhard says that something is still going on, and that the whole process is not at an end. We are in the process. Evolution has not reached its peak. We are on the way. And then? What is beyond man, what is ahead of us? I said we were at the top, we were the aim, the goal, the telos\ Yes! Up till now! And then? Something is happening through us, in us, with us, to complete the process. The process is still to be achieved. What is beyond man? Superman, James Bond? No! Something much better! Not even something like E.T. coming from another planet with a huge head and tiny feet. Horrible!

What is the superman to come? Teilhard does not speak at all of a superman but of ONE MAN, ONE BEING! A man of flesh, a synthesis of all humankind. The totality of humanity in one being. It is this synthesis of humanity beyond us, ahead of us, at the end of history. The end of this process Teilhard calls: Omega! Omega is the last letter of the Greek alphabet. Teilhard uses this letter to say that at the end of the process there is an Omega point which finalizes the whole process, and will bring the end of history, the end of mankind in a land of new mutation of the cosmos. Now I will explain what I mean by that:

Just as each grain of matter holds life within itself, each grain of life holds man in itself. We are human molecules, and inside of us Omega is at work. Omega is at work in each of us as a dream we hold within ourselves. If you ask me, "Father Boulad, do you have a dream?" I say:

"Yes, I have a dream! OMEGA!"

Omega is in me like a baby in its mother's womb, it is formation, it is expectation, pushing ahead. Each human being has a vocation to become Omega. I will not manage to become Omega on my own. In order to realize Omega, we need a new element which is superhuman, just as life has been able to synthesize matter because it is beyond matter! In order to synthesize matter in a tree, in a flower, you need something which is not material. Material plus material does not achieve synthesis. Life achieves a synthesis of matter. Man achieves a synthesis of life.

What is this new element which is going to achieve the synthesis of human kind? What is this Omega? For Teilhard it is a living person whom we call Christ, the son of man and the son of God who appeared in history and who will bring about this unity of mankind. That is why this historical man called Jesus Christ gave us ONE commandment, ONE law: love one another! All religions bring forth many commandments and lots of laws. Moses brought ten or more! Jesus spoke to us:

"This is my commandment: Love!"

He means love which brings together in one entity, the human molecules in order to build up the body, the body to come, future humanity, this Omega point. An interesting point is that St. Paul, in his Epistles, speaks about a kind of Omega in the shape of the Mystical Body, a body encompassing everything, grouping mankind to one, and reaching its completion at the end of history. Strange that through a scientific vision of evolution we should find such concepts as Christ's Mystical Body - Omega Point!

Teilhard's Christ is a cosmic Christ, a gigantic Christ. He is beyond all imagination. This Omega point is going to synthesize itself not only mankind here and now, you and me, but all humanity which came before and which is still to come! The whole cosmos and all life! It's like a kind of huge wave which started long, long, ago and will culminate in the living Christ at the end of history! But through man, through us! This is the point I would like to stress now!

We accomplish the first steps of Omega through our activity, through microphones, medias, books, through aeroplanes, metros, factories, schools, universities. Through all his activities, man is bringing together the elements of the cosmos and building them up, by himself, into a complete system. Internet was included among Teilhard's visions! 60 years ago! He had a certain vision of Internet as a kind of neural system, like man's neural system: these connecting nerves, within a system which unites the whole body with the brain. Teilhard de Chardin thought that there would soon be a kind of Internet bringing together all mankind in one synthesis. So our work, our activities, are preparing this unity of mankind which is to come and for which we are responsible.

(Ref I)

You ask about the possibility of extra-terrestrial beings below man or beyond man. We can have two opinions. Teilhard de Chardin's opinion is that on other planets in this extremely vast universe, it is most probable that there are spiritual beings different from man, either further or less developed than we are, because of the law of complexity conscience. The more complexity you have, the more conscience you get. So, the state of matter, and therefore of evolution can be more advanced on some other planets which do not belong to our solar system! Our solar system has no other beings, not even primitive life, but given the vastness of the universe, we surely have thousands if not millions of planets able to bear life.

Another possibility is that the earth is the only point in the whole universe on which a spiritual life has developed. We are the winners of a huge lottery, and the price has been won by the human race on planet earth. According to the anthropic principle, it's only on this small planet that the chances have been so great (a scientific miracle) that spiritual beings have been able to develop. We still don't know which of the two is true, which is the real perspective. I myself don't know! I agree completely that there could be extra-terrestrial beings according to the law I spoke about, and it may also be that the anthropic principle proves to be right.

In either case, what is the role of Christ and the Omega Point? Here there are also two positions. The traditional position is that the Incarnation of the Logos took place once and forever for the whole cosmos in Jesus of Nazareth. He is the only possible Incarnation of the Logos, and through him, through his Incarnation and Death on the Cross, the redemption of all the cosmos was achieved. This is the traditional position. Some theologians today question this position. They say that if there are other worlds with extraterrestrial beings in other galaxies, why couldn't the Logos not have had other Incarnations, on other planets, for other beings beyond our earth! The same Logos! The same Logos which became Jesus Christ on our Earth could have taken on a different shape through different Incarnations on different planets! In that case you would have different Christs, but the same Logos achieving the evolutionary movement towards one Omega Point.

I'll tell you my opinion: I am searching, I don't have a ready-made answer and I don't think theology can give a definite and clear-cut answer to this problem.

(Ref J)

Whether you like it or not, whether you know it or not, whether you understand it or not, whether you accept it nor not - Jesus Christ is the centre, the core, the kernel of humanity and of yourself as an individual. He is living in you even though you may not know or understand it. Some day you may recognize the fact - or never. He is living and acting and loving within you. But from the moment of grace, when you realize it fully, you will experience a 'surplus' in your life .

Here is an example: You have been in trouble and a kind stranger contacts you anonymously, gives you a lot of good advice, sends you one thousand dollars to get you out of your mess - but he hides himself, hides his name and his face. A mystery! After standing on your own feet again, you ask yourself who this hidden person was. Why was he so interested in your situation? How and why did he understand the story? Why did he save you? Why? Who is he? And after a long time of hopeless asking and searching for him, the doorbell rings, you open the door, and a person says to you: "Here I am." Your normal reaction would be to let him enter your house, in order to get to know more about him and to show him your gratitude for his goodness. Right?

Here is another example: You are carried away from the beach by the waves of a stormy lake, your life is in danger, you have already swallowed water, you are fainting and are about to drown. But a stranger appears, comes and saves your life. He brings you to the beach, but disappears immediately. After some time, having recovered, you open your eyes and see people around you who tell you about the unknown person who saved you at the risk of his own life. Is it not natural that you are longing to get to know him, to meet him, to thank him? So you make an effort to find out his name and his address until you have found him and learned more about him. You don't do this in order to gain another new life or anything else, not at all, that has been done already, you have been saved by him.

And another example: A king had twin sons, but one of them disappeared mysteriously at a very early age. Fortunately, he had a birthmark, on account of which he was found after fifteen years of searching among the poorest of the poor. The king went to visit him and revealed to him the truth of his royal descent. For some reason, he could not come home to his father's castle immediately, but the promise of his return was given him, also the reunion with his twin brother, and the inheritance of the kingdom one day. From that day on, the life of the poor boy changed dramatically. Now he knew his true father and his true home, and became keen to learn everything about the king of the country. And little by little he began to love him and to long for him.

This is the answer to the often-heard question: "Why preach the Gospel and why do such an enormous amount of apostolic work in the world? People are already saved, it's already accomplished - so why continue?" Whether he realizes it or not, everybody is saved by Jesus. We know the teaching of the Church, but apostolic work is a Revelation. It reveals the person who has saved him. Apostolic work is revealing the name of the Saviour. And this changes one's life completely; one acquires a new dimension through this knowledge, through this new faith and the awareness of this fact.

So the hidden action of Christ within each human being is a real act - some know about it, some don't. And those who do know want to proclaim it to the others who don't know it yet, or refuse to understand - Revelation! When we try to convey the Jesus' message to others we don't say: "Please listen, if you don't believe in Jesus you cannot be saved." No! No! ... Instead we say: "My friend, you are saved by Jesus, this is certain, but don't you want to know a bit more about the person who is so deeply interested in your fate? Don't you want to establish personal contact with him, and have a relationship with him - through prayer, through meditation, through learning?" This is the point.

Knowing and accepting Jesus as the Saviour means developing a new dimension in one's -life. That is why revelation and faith add something essential to life. I don't think it's a question of going to or not going to Heaven. This was the teaching and fear in the past, but that is all over since the Second Vatican Council (1962-1967). We have clear and beautiful texts about that. Whoever is honest with himself and lives in righteousness and faith - he is saved. My opinion is: what we call Christian Baptism is not "making" us God's sons and daughters, it is revealing to us what we are in our essence: children of God. And apostolic work helps people recognize it, to become aware of it, in order to be able to accept it freely.

Each human being - whether he is a Hindu, a Buddhist, a Jew, a Moslem or whatever he may be by birth and heritage - who listens to his conscience, and is faithful to it, who is really faithful to his own Self - is saved by Jesus. Why? Because he has accepted the LOGOS, the word of God, which speaks within each heart. He has just not yet recognized that this Logos has become incarnated in Jesus of Nazareth, so he does not know that the Logos is Jesus. He is not to blame for that. He is saved in a mysterious way through Jesus without knowing him. ***(Ref A)***

The Incarnation – when God becomes Man, becomes flesh – becomes a kind of necessity for me, a necessity because I cannot imagine God staying in heaven while people are suffering on earth. To love is to share, otherwise there is no love.

Sometimes we think that God has only come to save us from our sins. I may disagree with this formula. Why? I think that God has come, firstly to be with us, to share our faith, to share our life, to share all our suffering -for me this is the very reason for what we call Incarnation. And this is why, from the very beginning of his life, he is called Emmanuel, which means God with us. When we ask in connection with the war in Kosovo "Where is God?" my answer is that he is with the people who are dying, he is suffering with each one of them, he is one of the wounded people, with a child in arms, looking for shelter and food. When you watch television, and when you notice the faces of people trying to escape the bombs and weapons, I invite you to look carefully at their faces, and try to discover Christ's face in theirs. This is my invitation to you today, because he has told us: "I was persecuted and you will be persecuted as well." "I am the people escaping, I am the refugee from Kosovo, I am with you here - I am not in heaven." Faith is the act by which we discover God's face in a human face.

Now I would like to draw your attention to the meaning of Ascension. We say that Jesus came to Bethlehem, went to Nazareth, walked through Palestine, and after thirty-three years he was crucified in Jerusalem. Then he arose again and ascended into heaven. That's it. NO! There is no goodbye with Jesus. Ascension has to be understood in a completely different way than the way we think of it. Ascension is not Jesus going to heaven, Jesus' features, taking on a new form of presence, a new kind of presence among us and this explains his last words before the Ascension to his disciples: "I am with you all days until the end of time". Jesus, you are not logical, because you leave, and at the same time you say you are staying with us. Are you going or are you staying? He is not leaving. He came to dwell with us, to remain with us, to stay with us until the end of the world. He didn't escape to heaven, separated from us. The story of heaven is over. So, where is Jesus? Here on earth, in us, with us, in Kosovo, in Sudan, in Angola, in all the places where people suffer. Jesus is here. His name is Emmanuel.

(Ref S)

Chapter 3: The Church and Change

Vatican II was pure grace. But the problem was that people had to swallow at once 400 years of church history within four years of this council. For centuries, we had repeated certain dogmas which were then turned upside down overnight, like eating and drinking before Mass, for example. Before that, when I had a shower and I swallowed a drop of water inadvertently, I had to cough and spit out. When I was to celebrate Mass in the afternoon somewhere, I had to fast all day beforehand, and even in summer, in the heat of Egypt, a glass of water was forbidden for a priest ... This is just one example and there are countless others. But when this picture of the Church suddenly changed, many people were completely at a loss. Pope John XXIII was a prophet and a gift to our century as everybody agrees, but the Popes Paul VI and John Paul II decided to have a kind of restoration for the sake of the obviously troubled average person. In our present situation you have two kinds of Christians - those who are fully in agreement with Vatican II and even preparing silently Vatican III, and those who are still dreaming of Vatican I.

Vatican II does not only mean new laws, other dogmas, but first and foremost A NEW SPIRIT which began to blow through the Catholic Church. It was the first council which was not against somebody or something, but for something! The Church has had to undergo a complete change, deep, deep inside herself, but so far this has not been achieved. On the contrary, we are at the beginning of this development. I say development, but in reality Vatican II is a renewed consciousness and a return to the true Gospel, to the true Spirit of our origins. This Spirit confronts Man with his absolute responsibility towards his own conscience. Many Christians have been raised and treated like kids and to this day, most of them are kept at the mental age of a child. The Church was pleased and satisfied about her obedient flock, and any member asking deeper questions or searching was naughty, and quickly called an 'atheist'. Doubters, who were often profound seekers, were automatically considered outsiders, they no longer belonged to the community. However, in every age there have been, within the Church, serious believers who did not agree with this or that, yet they remained faithful to Mother Church and never revolted against her. Silently, they were longing and praying for a change to come.

The question now is how to help Christians to reach adulthood with a sense of responsibility and with some knowledge. Should everything be repeated continuously in order to remain as it is forever? ... It is, unfortunately, the case that most Christians are still living at the level of a theological culture the size of the old catechism so to speak, and with the knowledge of a primary school child. They have never developed their Christian understanding and nobody inspired them to ask questions. And this is what is urgently needed today, this is what our apostolic work - sermons, discussion groups - should promote in a wholly new structure of the Church.

(Ref B)

The concept of the parish was inherited from the Middle Ages; it was a geographical parish, the parish in the centre and the people around it. Nowadays, the parish is no longer geographical. People come by bus and car to a parish, which may be far away from their home, because they like the priest, because they have friends there. The parish is no longer geographical. And, you have another kind of parish: the weekend parish. At the weekend people go elsewhere, to different places, they go to a church which is not their own, meet people they don't know.

What is a parish? What should a parish be? A parish is a living community in which people know each other, where they have real contacts, and experience togetherness. This was the case in the Middle Ages. Nowadays, if you take a big parish in a big city, you have one to five thousand or ten to twenty thousand people, with perhaps eight Franciscans or eight Jesuits or eight parish priests, knowing their parishioners by computer. I don't know if this is the case with you.

The point I am making is that even if only 800 go to church, the parish still consists of 11.000 people for whom the parish priest is responsible although most of them don't go to church. So more or less 8% practice here. And now to my suggestion: in a parish, first of all, people should know each other. There should be a living community, with a pastor "who knows his sheep and his sheep know him", as it is mentioned in the gospel. This is possible in a village of 300 people when the pastor has been there for a year or two. A normal person knows one or two hundred people well, in depth, but not more. The problem nowadays is that the parish does not lend itself to being a really close community with a human element. We have to reinvent the parish, but how....?

If I were the Pope I would divide the parish up, for example a parish of ten thousand people into one hundred parishes, each parish with a flock of one hundred people. You'll say we'll have to find one hundred pastors! Do you have them? Yes! How? Married priests! I come from the Middle East where all the Orthodox priests are married; they even have to marry before ordination. And in the Catholic Eastern rites they are free to choose between getting married or remaining celibate. Some decide to get married, so the bishop allows it when they have finished studying theology, and if, after five years, the marriage is stable, with evidence of a healthy family life and a good spiritual life, they can be ordained. This happens in our Catholic Churches of the East. Another possibility is that a married man with grown up children is longing for priesthood. He mentions this to the bishop, and the bishop tests him, and gives him a special training which is not the same as that in the seminary, but he will ordain him. In this way he can stay in his village or in his neighborhood, in his apartment with his family and insure his service to a given church, celebrating the Eucharist, etc.

In my new vision for .the parish, the church should call people to the priesthood. The old concept of vocation was built on the idea, 'I have a vocation.' which means that God is calling me to become a priest. Remember, this was not the case in the beginning. When St. Paul was founding new churches all over Asia Minor, Greece, Italy, he addressed certain chosen persons, mostly older men: 'I need you to be in charge of this community. Can you? Will you?' Then he put his hands upon his head and he ordained him to look after this small flock. Why not do the same as St. Paul today, what is the problem? I don't know why there is an obstacle for ordaining married people in the Latin Church. And I would ask any one of you who has raised his children, has free time, has no financial problems, to be the pastor of his block. A large building with twenty floors could become a parish; he could build a large hall which would be the meeting point for Sunday mass or other ceremonies, celebrations, discussion groups, conferences, lectures, etc. He would know the people of his building, knock at their door, have coffee with them, ask them how they are, note their birthdays, get to know them better and better. What kind of people? Never mind, they probably don't go to church, have no religious education, but gradually he would create a human relationship among them, and this human community would gradually become a Christian community; this is the secret and this is the promise.

The split between the human community and the Christian community is wrong. In Africa, South America and Asia they are rediscovering the basic Christian community, the parish is becoming a basic human community in which everything is shared and everybody knows everybody else. The head of this community is not a priest, he is a layman! The principle of ordaining married persons to lead a community - this is the future Church for me.

Another kind of community or parish can be a group of friends. A community based on friendship, is a parish. What usually happens when you have a dinner or a family celebration, you invite people from different places? It is not a geographical community (1), or a weekend community (2), it is a community of friends (3). And the last kind of parish which is still unthinkable is the community in which you work (4). WHO FAO United Nations, firms, factories, banks, etc., you live and work together in a compound for five to fifteen years, this is a human community, and you have to think how you can make a Christian community out of this human community. This is not easy because you may have people of different faiths. My question is, has Christianity anything to do with Christianising a working place, an office, a factory? In answering, I refer to the Acts of the Apostles when I speak about the community, because in Chapter 4 you have the expression 'one heart and one soul'. The whole group of believers was united, heart and soul. (Acts 4, 32).

I would say that priesthood in this context would be twofold, married priesthood for established parishes and celibate priesthood for itinerant parish work, for nationwide or international work. I think we need two kinds of priests, those who have chosen celibacy freely would be mobile priests, able to move, be in charge of spiritual education in a whole diocese or a whole country. They have no wives and children so they are free to travel. We also need priests like this. We need priests at the level of international relations. It is very important for today's church to be present at UN Headquarters where international policy is being shaped.

(Ref C)

Faith cannot be lived outside the Church, but in the community. The community is essential for giving support to one's individual faith. We are sometimes unable to cope with events and circumstances which seem stronger than us. I dislike doctors (not as people) but at certain times I need a doctor or someone to help me, though I like to do things by myself. The community is there when you cannot manage your life by yourself, you need help. This is the meaning of the Church. Some people say: "I don't need the Church, I can encounter God alone and pray by myself." No, the Church is a necessity, we are social beings, not just individuals.

(Ref N)

In the past, the Church promised salvation only to her own members: Extra Ecclesiam Nulla Salus. There was no idea of salvation for non-Christians, not even for non-Catholics. Since Vatican II, the teaching is that the doors of heaven have been opened to the believers of other religions too. If they are faithful to their beliefs, if they follow their conscience and remain honest with themselves, they will be saved. Both the concepts of Baptism and Redemption have undergone this change. The whole Church is rethinking herself. Is the Church merely visible or does she go beyond her visibility? Are there more revelations in other Holy Scriptures beside the Christian message of the Bible?

(Ref Q)

If every human being can be saved by following his own religion and his own conscience, then why do we preach the Gospel, why do we indoctrinate, why do we convert? We now have to rethink what it means to be a Christian. Karl Rahner speaks about 'the anonymous Christian', meaning that every human being who is faithful to himself is Christian without knowing it. Catholics believe that Jesus Christ is the only way to salvation, the only door between this world and the one beyond. Why? Because Christ is fully God AND fully Man. The realm of God and the realm of Man are totally united in this Person, born in Bethlehem. Therefore his is the door to what we call God. This is what he said about himself:

"I am the Way, the Truth, and the Life:
No one can come to the Father except through me.
If you know me you know my Father too.
From this moment you know him and have seen him."
(John 14, 6-7)

For a Christian, Christ is the only way. In the past, in order to be a believer, you had to be baptised. Nowadays it is no longer necessary to join this sociological and institutional body called Church in order to be saved. St. John has the following to say about Jesus:

"The Word is the true light
that enlightens all men
and he was coming into the world."
(John 1,9)

This inner light coming to Christians, to Buddhists, to Moslems and to all mankind is the Logos which manifested itself in Jesus. You can believe in Jesus as the historical figure who lived two thousand years ago, or you can follow your true inner light faithfully, thus partaking in the mystery of salvation in Jesus. The question is no longer who will or will not be saved, because we now believe that every human being who in all honesty follows his conscience can be saved, whatever his religion is. What, then, makes Christianity so important to us? What can it add to the other religions? Christianity reveals to us the depth and extent of God's love for mankind which already manifested itself in the Old Testament and culminated in the Person of Jesus. Jesus reveals God to us, not up in heaven, but God down here among us, sharing life with us. From being a great philosophical concept, God now becomes a reality, speaking to us, guiding us, suffering with us. This is what we call Christian Revelation.

If we imagine God as a lonely being, far away from us in the heavens, all-powerful, ruling the universe according to his will, can we then speak of him as a God of love? Yes or no? Christians nowadays have to rediscover their God. I am sorry, but I doubt if they know him. They have to rediscover this God of love who leaves heaven in order to share our destiny, this God of love who cannot remain in peace on high and far away from us. Not only did he send us prophets and Books of Revelation, as the Muslims and Jews say, but, as St. John proclaimed:

"Yes, God loved the world so much,
that he gave his only Son,
so that everyone who believes in him
may not be lost
but may have eternal life."
(John 3, 16)

He came to share our lives, our suffering, and our death. And he remains within us, he is Emmanuel. In coming, he identified himself with each of us. When we pray: "Our Father who is in Heaven", heaven is not up there, but down here, in us, and for ever. In order to discover God and to be united with him, we do not have to escape from this world but sink deep down into ourselves, into our lives, into one another, until we find this Existential God in our own world.

I believe that this Existential God is the answer to the religious quest of our modern world. Whether religions cling to their past — and this is a dead end for me because you cannot revive what is long past — or look forward. Religions can only survive by a deepening of their spiritual experience of God. I call this important spiritual experience mysticism. Mysticism is a personal encounter with God, taking place deep inside me, and has something to do with love.

There are three kinds of mysticism: the Monistic, the Theistic and the Christian. Hindu and Buddhist mysticism are monistic. What does this mean? Monos comes from Greek and means 'one'. There is only one Supreme Being. The individual merges with this Ultimate Being in a kind of total self-denial, the person fades and dissolves into Nirvana. There is no reality outside the Supreme Being, Brahma. We humans are non-existent beings, we are maya, we are just illusions. In Theistic Mysticism, the ultimate reality is at least a person. Islam is a theistic religion: through prayer, the believer can get in touch with a personal God, an infinite Being, an absolute God who is a living person, but far beyond him, unattainable since time immemorial.

But in Christian Mysticism, the God you meet in your soul is not only a divine Person, he is more. He is Love which is revealed to us in Jesus Christ. Through his life and death, through his words and deeds, Jesus has disclosed to us God's true nature, has lifted the veil of secrecy and made himself known to Mankind. Not totally, of course! Who will ever grasp his mystery? He has revealed to us that we are not only creatures but Children of God. In Islam, human beings are called 'abid' which is the plural of habt' and means 'slaves'. Human beings are called 'slaves of God' in Arabic, and Christ says we are no longer `servants' but friends' and 'children of God'. This deep form of union between God and Mankind is different from all the other forms of union we know.

I think that in the future, all religions should open themselves to mysticism. This was not the case in the past. Islam banned Moslem mysticism, the Sufis were persecuted because they strayed from strict Islamic orthodoxy. Some great Christian mystics have been suspected of heresy and were condemned. Today there is such a great emptiness, a lack of mysticism in our Catholic and Protestant Churches that many Christians are turning towards Asian mysticism. In order to be relevant to modern Man, religion must stop being a structure that functions well in a liturgical frame. It must enter real life again. Most people do not want to go to church, to the mosque or to the temple just to perform their religious duty, nor do they want religion imposed on them.

But they need spiritual nourishment
they crave for answers,
they long for experience.

Religious feeling lives deeply within human nature, and all it needs to be brought forth is a revitalised existential religion of Life And Love.

(Ref Q)

The Church has to invent a new language. This is urgent. Let us abandon the complicated theology during Mass! How many of the listeners know enough to be able to follow? Who has knowledge of the dogmas? No, what we need is a meaningful language for people, connected to their daily lives, spoken from the heart to hearts. Existential! The whole parish of today has to be re-thought, re-felt, re-built. It is urgent!

(Ref B)

Chapter 4
Suffering, Death and the After-life

I want to consider the creative energy of suffering. A woman called Denise Legrix was born without feet, without legs, without hands, without arms. *Born like that* is the title of a book (Paris 1968). Yes, she was born like that, that is to say: a torso with a head. This woman, who lived through terrible moments, has been able to overcome her despair and then launched an appeal through Radio Luxembourg for the foundation of a "Centre for the Handicapped". This woman, who is a symbol of helplessness itself, without hands or feet, with only a mouth, has used this mouth and has spoken and dictated two books. She has spoken on the television and on the radio. Denise Legrix has founded a National Institute for Rehabilitation and a National Foundation For Convalescents. She has opened 4 establishments: A home "Denise Legrix", a home for Neurologiques, a home for Motor-Cerebral Disabilities and an Outpatient Clinic - all for several million Francs. This woman, who could have said:

"I have nothing to offer in this world, I am an outcast of society; all I am capable of is to live in a hospice and have other people look after my every need," has created an institution, a photo of which you will find on her book - a magnificent building - with nothing, but nothing - but with her will power.

And when I see so many people who have arms and legs, who have everything they need yet do not know what to do with their life, who drag their way through an empty existence asking "what shall I do?", people who have achieved or created nothing worthwhile - and then I see this woman who started such an extraordinary undertakings . When I meet so many who have everything but do not know what to make of their existence, and compare them with this woman who could so easily have abandoned herself to despair, but throw herself into this remarkable work.

Suffering is an obstacle only to those who wish to give up. Suffering can be a creative energy for him who can face up to it and overcome it. Then the creative force of suffering begins to work in him. In Cairo, at The Institute For The Blind, I met a man who had lost his sight in the Second World War, a man who, he too, had despaired. He had been treated in England - without success; then he returned to Cairo and established an Institute For The Blind, which I have visited myself. This man told me his story and said:

"When I plumbed the depths of despair, it was then that I

realised that one must be stronger than despair, and

I threw myself into doing something positive."

These examples are the proof that the Chinese proverb is true:

"MAN IS THE SON OF THE OBSTACLE".

I found in the French magazine *PARIS MATCH* a picture of a young woman of 26 years. She had been a champion of riding and swimming. One day, due to a miscalculation, she dived into water which was too shallow and broke her spine. This girl too, passed months of anguish and despair, tied to her bed, paralysed for the rest of her life. Her name is Jonnie Ericson. She also was able to overcome her despair and taught herself to draw and paint, holding the brush with her teeth. Now she paints postcards and pictures and sells them and earns her living. But not only does she earn her living, she has refound her faith and she has refound her joy, and she has refound a marvellous smile. She signs all her cards:

" P.T.L. "   (PRAISE THE LORD) ,

and she holds meetings for young Americans who crowd around her, on the meaning of life, on happiness and on faith.

To believe that misfortune, suffering, pain, can destroy a person, is not to know that there exist in man undreamt-of powers of resurrection which are capable of propelling him into a new dimension, undreamt-of, because he did not even know it existed, and it is that suffering which brings these powers forth from the very depth of his being.

I have given you these examples of the creative energy of suffering on perhaps a rather "superficial" level. Denise Legrix has founded a great work, buildings were constructed and money collected: that appeals to our imagination. The other has founded an Institute for the Blind. The young girl Jonnie Ericson gives onferences, creates cards. But I want to reach with you a deeper level, because suffering creates and builds something, not so much on the surface but deep inside us. I believe that suffering is a condition of self-realisation and of self-awareness.

Man, before his birth, is purely coincident with himself. In his mother's womb he is at one with himself, and, if I may say so, it is his heaven on earth. The mother's womb has always been seen by psychiatrists as the image, the prototype, the symbol, the dream of that paradise in which man lives before his birth and which he seeks to find again.

Well, this paradise is an animal paradise. Man in that state is a small animal; not that he is not already a man - do not make me say what I do not mean - but he is in the state of an animal which has not yet achieved self-awareness. What Must He Do To Achieve Self-Awareness?

It is by breaking away something! It is by a series of successive detachments, that a man will achieve the distance from himself, which is necessary for him to reach self-realisation as a true human being. As long as man is purely coincident with himself there can be no humanity. First must come the experience of birth (the first detachment from the maternal bosom). He will later form a fresh attachment to his mother by taking her milk. Then he must be weaned (second detachment) to cleave him from his mother. And each one is painful, but each one is a step towards development, towards self-awareness. Later he reaches the OEDIPUS phase, but he must outgrow this selfish love for the parent of the opposite sex, he must outgrow once more the two-fold situation, to reach the "triangular" situation (third detachment). At a certain age he must go to school and leave the family circle (fourth detachment).

It is thus, by successive detachments, that the child grows psychologically, that he achieves the necessary distance from himself by which he becomes a person. To become a person is unceasingly to tear one-self away from what one already is in order to become what one is called to be.

Once a man stops himself, once a man settles down, once a man is bogged down in what he is, or in what he believes himself to be, in the comfortable security of his environment, his family circle or his profession, at that moment he is a dead man. It is because of this that the Lord sends us, from time to time, a detachment. Everything which tears us away from what we are, from how we live, from our tranquility, all this makes us grow. There is no self awareness without pain, for every detachment is pain. But this is the way to our self-realisation.

There is at the beginning of man's existence, an identification of man with his false "I". The "I", that which I am, is never something which is given, it is something which becomes, something which emerges. Therefore as long as I identify with my "I" of today and of now - I die. I am a being which is blocked, paralysed, arrested in my development. Therefore, so that I do not identify with my "I", so that I can transcend it to arrive at that "BEING" which I am called to become I must - without ceasing - overcome myself.

Now, this overcoming of one's self is achieved by a detachment from everything I possess: from my body, my life, from my liberty'. All this means suffering, because man tends always to identify with himself,that is to say with his body and his liberty, his house and possessions. Each detachment permits us to release our true personality, our true being.

Therefore the life of man is a continual rebirth, he is never finished with being born.... birth is not the unique moment when an existence commences. To ourselves we are born every day. To be born is a process without end. The first de-detachment is but a first step towards something else, thus this succession of births, which is a succession of deaths, for to be born is to die and to die is to be born.

For those among you who read French, may I refer to two brochures, a summary of the conferences which I gave in Europe on the mystery of death. To be born is to die and to die is to be born. These are two phases of the same reality, that is to say that suffering is identically growth, and death is identically birth, until the second birth, which is called the true death. The true death is the accession to our final being, there where we have left behind us all we possess. For at the moment we die, what is it that emerges, what is it that lingers, what is it that is left? Nothing but the pure and naked essence of the being. My being, my Self, in order to free itself totally, must lose everything - and this is the last detachment.

Therefore I would say that everything which leads to this detachment must be viewed from its positive aspect, from its constructive aspect, and it is this, the role of suffering that reveals man to himself. We know this phrase of Jesus:

"What is born of the flesh is flesh,

what is born of the Spirit is spirit". (John 3, 6)

This small body which is born of the flesh is still flesh, it is not yet "Me". Man must be reborn, therefore this first birth is in itself nothing at all. An animal also is born as a man is, there is no difference between the birth of a small dog and the birth of a man. The process is exactly the same. The difference is that for man this birth is only a starting point for something more. So it is by this process which enables him to become himself that man achieves self-realization. He receives his self from himself, he creates himself.

You may know these verses of Alfred De Musset :

"Man is an apprentice, pain is his master,
And no-one knows himself until he has suffered.
It is a hard law, but a supreme law, ancient as the world and fate,
which we must, to our sorrow, receive as a baptism,
And it is at this sad price that all must be bought."

No-one knows himself until he has suffered"... No, we cannot know ourselves until we have undergone suffering. We cannot know who we are until we have undergone this experience of suffering. To suffer is to discover oneself. There is no self-awareness, there is no self-knowledge, without this painful experience, "which we must, to our sorrow, receive as a baptism" ... Suffering understood as a baptism! And what is a baptism in the Christian sense of the word?

A baptism is a death and a resurrection. It is an immersion in the water that is, at the same time, death and life. By saying that suffering is death in emphasizing its positive aspect, I do not wish to obliterate or neglect its negative aspect, please understand. There is a death, but that death is life itself. These are two phases of the same phenomenon, to the extent that one can say with Descartes "I think, therefore I am":

I SUFFER, THEREFORE I AM.

For man, "to be" is to be able to live through this suffering with a certain attitude which we will speak about later. I suffer, therefore I am. The Self detaches itself at this depth of suffering, for pleasure is coincident of the body, as a body to the earth and to nature. Pleasure identifies us with this natural world from which we have sprung and all "pleasure in life" returns us to the "animal state" at the beginning of our existence.

Not that all pleasure is necessarily bad, for we are still animal in a small part of ourselves, and I hope that Aristotle is right when he says "man is a reasoning animal"... So this part which is animal exists, it cannot be denied, and pleasure exists and has its place in our life. But pleasure is coincident to the body, it is coincident to nature. Therefore as far as we live at the level of pleasure - there is no emergence of man in the full sense. Man does not emerge as a real person by only the experience of pleasure. Only by distance from it a part of humanity grows.

It is always the same idea which keeps recurring until the moment when the distance becomes so great that all ties are broken and death comes, that there is complete emergence of man. Thus, this distance with regard to pleasure of which we speak, becomes greater and becomes finally total, definitive. It becomes radical in the phenomenon of death, which is the total emergence of the being as a person, as a true human being.

Another aspect of suffering: suffering purifies man in the sense that it liberates him, that it enables him to discover the essential. One suffers, and many things which seemed very important lose their significance. Suffering merely gives entry into a truth, the truth of our BEING. It frees us from illusion and in this sense it purifies us.

One can compare suffering to a block of marble chiselled by the sculptor. We are, at birth, a block without form and contours, without a face, without significance. The chisel of the sculptor must chip away piece by piece: each piece which falls from the block is something of ourselves which is removed. One has the impression of losing something important, but that which is lost is won, because what must be revealed is precisely that statue which is hidden beneath.

What we lose is the inessential and what remains is the essential.

And I think that this comparison of the statue is very revealing to our understanding because there is much in us which has to be lost: ... I would like to quote to you a phrase by Georges Bernanos in *The Dialogue of The Carmelites*: A nun says to her Mother Superior:

"Oh, Reverend Mother, when I think how many things I have to reach!"

"You should say: to lose!" replied the Reverend Mother. Perfection is often perceived as something to be attained, to be acquired. I am going to acquire virtue, I am going to acquire excellence, I am going to acquire something or other.

And the Lord makes me understand very soon in my spiritual life that it is not so much a question of acquiring something as of losing something, of losing a lot of things ...The spiritual life is a progressive simplification of the being until it reaches a state of total simplicity.

Christ says:

"I tell you solemnly, unless you change and become like little children you will never enter the kingdom of heaven." (Matth.18,3)

Return to childhood!... It is this simplicity, a simplicity recovered, rediscovered, rewon by the simplicity of a child. It is a simplicity which rediscovers childhood, it is a childhood refound and not a childhood perpetuated. So it is a matter of losing many things, to become oneself. We are burdened indeed, and when the Lord wishes to help us he frees us from those burdens. He allows a thief to steal your wallet from your pocket or something else. That has happened to me five or six times, and each time I realized that it was a good thing I lose things or I have health problems or other difficulties, but each time I understand that the Lord has done well, very well! And in this way, if we open our eyes, if we open our ears, if we open our heart, we understand. We understand that there is always a gain, and the loss is only apparent.

My loss at a certain level is a gain at another level.

Suffering is also a warning. It is an alarm bell. A sick man who does not suffer is a man who is dangerously ill because there is no alarm bell called suffering which makes him cry . But when he cries "ouch!" the doctor finds out what the reason is. But when a sick man feels nothing, from this moment the bad can triumph and spread. Suffering is a vital warning and the Lord has deliberately put this warning in the organism to awaken man, to put him in a state of alert. An organism which does not suffer is an organism which is truly in danger. It is a defensive reaction in the face of peril.

I would like to mention an experiment which was completed in the United States in 1978. It was the result of 10 years of research. You know very well that the capacity of intelligence is in direct relation to the surface of the brain, that is to say that the brain is coiled round itself inside the skull and presents a very large surface area. The more it is twisted the greater the surface area, and it is at its maximum in man who develops.

At the University of California scientists have examined the cortex of different animals - rats, mice, cats, dogs, monkeys - that have been tortured for a very long time in the laboratory while experiments were made on them, which you know. Finally, after the death of these animals which have suffered enormously, their brains were examined and it was found that brain development was highly advanced and it showed a much higher level of intelligence. This is a proof, I would say biologically, that suffering develops the cerebral cortex and makes the creature more intelligent. This scientific experiment illustrates a reality, that is: suffering opens the spirit to new realities, it opens the intelligence.

Of course we are not speaking of an intelligence which is identified with mathematics and the sciences. The intelligence here is that which is capable of understanding the essence of things , the mystery of existence, the mystery of life and death, the mystery of man, aspiration intelligence which penetrates the very heart of the being.

There is the American Jesuit Father Walter Young and some years ago he was struck down by haemoplegia in a matter of seconds. He under-went treatment and now walks very painfully with the aid of two walking sticks. All one side of his body is paralysed. He was talking with me this summer and he said: "If I loved someone, really loved him, I would wish him to live through what I have lived through. The greatest blessings which God has given me in my life is to have sent me this." He had discovered, through his terrible handicap a new dimension of himself and his being that otherwise he would never have suspected.

Sometimes it saddens me to see people who have never suffered. There are faces among us which are beatifically happy, I almost said stupidly happy. They look at me and I know that they have never suffered, not in their body, not in their heart. Ah well! These are "poor" people, they have no depth, they cannot understand. Many things of our human existence those people will never understand. "no-one knows the mystery of man as long as he has not suffered."

There is in the world at present a determination to suppress suffering: childbirth without pain, operations without pain, the simple treatment by a dentist without pain, aspirin and tranquilizers for everything and morphine is also available for everybody. They want to suppress pain and suffering, they want to wipe out the tragedies of life. They must be hidden. Life through rose-coloured spectacles seen as a rose-coloured life. But life is not rose-coloured! Try to hide from children the right colour of life and wait and see! Why hide from children? Why hide an accident, why hide that someone in the family has died?

I am thinking of the United States where death is beautified, a pretty make up, a pretty dress, a beautiful room and they come and say: "See how handsome he is!" or "How lovely she looks!" They want to remodel the face of death. They want to pretend he (or she) is not dead, they want to show that death does not exist, that he (or she) is still alive. They want to forget that death is death and that it is decay, mouldering, burial, separation, that death is a tearing away. It is all this, let's face it!

I much prefer the Moslems, who bury their dead in a shroud in the sand, just like that! That is much better, because that is the truth. Naked you came from the body of your mother, naked you will return to the heart of the earth with this shroud as your only vestment and nothing more. That is the truth.

We cannot disguise death; we must look it in the face and look suffering in the face also. It is not to say that they may not be anesthetised! When I was in hospital I was very glad indeed that they anesthetised me. And yet, at the same time, I don't know... in anesthetising a man one dulls a certain sensitivity in him, a certain delicacy, a certain capacity to feel things which are, maybe, important.

Our ancestors, no-one anesthetised them. Saint Ignatius of Loyola, when his leg was broken by a cannon ball the surgeons of those days arrived with their hammer and their saw and their screwdriver to put his leg, without any anaesthetics, back into shape. He had suffered death and it is perhaps that which converted him later. Founder of the Jesuit Orders and finally a Saint!

When one arrives in a country, by means, of tranquillisers, of social security, of perfect hospitals and hygiene in everyone's daily life, then one arrives at the same time at a situation which is tragic. One realises: when tragedy is eliminated from existence it reappears in another form - to the point that the latest statistics from Switzerland, the most "sterilised" country in the world, show that the number of suicides last year was higher than the number of deaths from road-accidents. One cannot eliminate tragedy from existence. Existence is tragic and, from his earliest days, a child must become used to seeing that touching tragedy, to living tragedy. Death is a companion with whom we must travel each day, so that when it confronts us on the last day, we can say, like Saint Francis:

"Blessings on you, death, my friend, my brother!"

But we do not know how to say this phrase. We live in a modern world and in full progress. But what progress? What progress? We do not even know how to behave beside a hospital bed or at funerals, as they say, we make a "funeral face". That does not mean we should laugh at funerals, but that is something else again... There is a profundity in death which we have to look in the face and we have to learn that for a long time so that it becomes familiar. All suffering is a little death and it prepares us for the great death.

A man who suffers no more returns to the foetal condition, that is to say the condition which I spoke of just now, which is the origin itself of man in his animality, who is that person I spoke of with a beaming face, "Ces bourgeois épanouis" as Gustave Flaubert called them.

I am thinking of this famous Lebanese author Taha Hussein... He would never have been Taha Hussein if he had not lost his sight at an early age. Taha Hussein would never have written "Le Livre des Jours", that extraordinary book, if he had not lost his sight. What made Taha Hussein great was precisely that loss, it has created him, it is that which formed him, it is that which made him great. That which makes one great is suffering, otherwise one is not yet great...

At the side of a hospital bed I feel small, very small! This patient who is lying here, it is he who is great: curled up there, it is he who is greater than me! Suffering makes greatness that we do not understand, because we are mesmerised by other greatnesses. I would say that man so long as he has not suffered, has only two dimensions, he is like a picture which has only two dimensions. Suffering adds the important third dimension, the dimension of depth. A human being who has suffered, you submerge yourself in him, you know there are depths in him, something more, something hidden. This regard is not like the others! Oh, we have certain ideas on strength and on weakness, on greatness and smallness, which are different.

He who is strong, can be very weak, and he who is weak is strong.

And now I am going to speak about Magda. She is 39 years old and she is completely paralysed since she was 11 years old. She has neither brothers nor sisters, and her parents died a long time ago. She lives in the International Old People's Home in Alexandria/Moharrem-Bey with the terminal sick and the old people. At the beginning of her admission it was very hard for her to resign herself. She screamed and fought for a whole summer, but little by little she understood and accepted. Each time I go there to see these old people and say Mass for the Sisters, I see her, Magda, her shining face, her marvellous smile: when she sees me and she tries hard to say something, but she cannot speak anymore, and she cannot move her hands, nor her arms and legs. At the age of 39 years and since 11 years she has been tied to her bed. You can go and see her, she will be pleased: and you will also be pleased to see the most beautiful smile not that of a film star, it is beautiful in another way, a smile which springs from a heart which has been completely transformed and purified by suffering. You can talk to her, she understands everything and will answer to you with her smiling eyes.

When I see Magda I feel so small: She is great, she is very great, she is heroic, she surpasses me immeasurably. She is in another sphere, in a higher dimension than I am. She became a child again, pure and simple. Magda has understood and accepted, what has happened to her.

Another aspect:
Suffering opens the heart to others,
Suffering helps understanding of others.

A short time ago someone came to see me. She was hard, authoritarian, very sure of herself, judging everyone with rigorous justice. And then it happened that this person had a misfortune which crushed her, but this new reality humiliated her in her great pride. From the height of her pedestal she fell low, very low in her own eyes, very low compared with the ideal image which she had made of herself. She spoke to me of this and I said to her: "This is the greatest blessing which the Lord has given you." She said: "But it is not possible that I, I, I...." "Yes., it is possible that you..... This way you will finally understand others, this way you will know what it is to be weak and fragile. In future you will know about that better." And after a while she confessed: "It's true what you say. I am much more indulgent, much more understanding of people now."

"No-one knows himself unless he has suffered".
And: no-one understands others unless he has suffered.

Among those who come to see me when I am in hospital, when I am sick and tired, I know those who have suffered much and those who have suffered little. It is a certain way of speaking and behaving, a certain way of looking and smiling. He who has suffered knows how to speak to an invalid, he knows how to visit and how to stay with him. This person has not learnt it in books, those are not things one learns in books. Suffering gives us a capacity of intuition, of delicacy, a sixth sense in dealing with others. We perceive realities which otherwise we would not comprehend. Suffering opens us up, opens our heart, breaks the shell of egoism which constantly shuts us in upon ourselves.

And when suffering falls upon a house in the form of a handicapped child, we all know of such a family, at first it is unbearable, they refuse it, they cannot accept it, they revolt. And then this child becomes a privileged way through which the family is uplifted, lives an extraordinary union. The child becomes the bond and the meeting-place of husband and wife, they are joined together by this child and both grow. I have known families which have been completely metamorphosised by the presence of a little child who suffers in their midst. It is he who has created the true family life. The creative energy of suffering..

Suffering opens up to ourselves. Suffering opens up to others. Suffering opens up to God. When a man sees such fragility, such precariousness, such helplessness, then he is able to transcend himself. Otherwise, man, the man of health and perfect strength, the man in full possession of his faculties, lives an auto-sufficiency which shuts him in upon himself.

"I am master of myself. The world is mine1 I need nobody to help me, so why God? I am sufficient unto myself. I have my money, my house, my car. What else do I need?"

But, but... when suffering brushes him with its wings and ties him to his bed and takes away some of his wealth - then something happens! At that moment he perceives a new reality to which he had never before given his attention. Now he discovers who is God, what is faith and what is the transcendence at the heart of his existence. He discovers new dimensions. How many people have been completely transformed by suffering! How many people have cast themselves into the arms of God! How many people have discovered true joy, the joy which is the fulfillment of that ascension of which I speak! Joy, true joy, something different from pleasure! You see, at the starting point, at the foetal stage, there is pure pleasure, and it is the total coincidence of the Self, the Self living in its complete animality. At the end there is joy. Between pleasure and joy lies the gulf we are speaking of. But for that ascension to come to pass there is but one condition: to accept our suffering, to take suffering upon ourselves. And this is not easy. The intellectuals in the West preach rebellion, and it is good form, it is fashionable to rebel, to rebel against everything, against authority, against God. God, that despot, that tyrant who amuses himself by torturing us...

But there are others who accept their suffering which they are unable to change in their faith. They understand at the moment they suffer, that there is a loving face bent over them. They know that in that face and in those loving eyes is the same suffering they are feeling themselves. As soon as they realise that truth, they are able to take the first step to overcome their rebellion. Rebellion achieves nothing. Rebellion exists only at a certain level, where one can still struggle. But one day one has to understand that it is greater and wiser to surrender, for you will give yourself into the arms of a father.

I believe that one does not understand suffering at once, but always afterwards. It is never before that one understands suffering. Do not try, as I am doing, to explain it right now. You will do it later when you have passed through and then you understand. That is why there must be an act of faith, so that you will realise and rediscover that other dimension: accept, surrender, take suffering upon yourself: And at that moment it becomes truly h u m a n , at that moment it becomes constructive. The suffering which creates can also destroy a person if one does not know how to accept it, if one struggles against it, if one resists and hardens oneself.

Suffering achieves something beyond the apparent, even when it restricts and weakens us. Something happens in the world which is called the great communion of men, that is to say that we are all, beyond the visible in communion with one another, by something more profound than our superficial ties. We are all branches of the same tree!

Try to imagine a tree in winter of which you can only see the summit. You see some branches and you do not see that those hundreds of branches below which emerge are all joined to a single trunk. All is one, and we are all a part of that one. You cannot perceive it, and yet it is the truth about mankind. In the same way you see more than two hundred people here in this conference room united for two hours tonight in Alexandria. You know, that some are going to Bulkeley after this conference, some to Mazarita, some to Roushdy and so on. It does not matter..., we separate, but we are all a link, one with the other, and essential. That is to say, a link which nothing can break, we are brothers, brothers one to the other in the deepest sense of the word. We are in communion and joined together, relating one to the other, in the most profound and intimate way. That is what is known as the mystical relationship, the mystical body of humanity, corpus mysticum.

That is the great mystery. Nothing is lost, nothing is ever lost of human pain, not an atom of suffering, not a single tear shed, not a cry of a child, not a moan of a dying person, not a death-rattle, nothing is lost in the emptiness of space.

ALL THIS IS A SEED FROM WHICH A TREE WILL GROW.

All is refound in the great gathering! The suffering that I experience at night in my bedroom in my solitude is a force which regenerates the world. My heart suffers but it creates an energy through which something grows somewhere on earth. Nothing is lost in our world, all is refound and saved.

This is a law as authentic as the physical laws of thermo dynamics which one learns at school and university. Nothing is lost in the physical world, as nothing is lost in the spiritual world. I spoke to you about Teilhard De Chardin and his vision of the world and about that famous anthropoid law which exists only at a certain level.

I explained how the law has another side, another face, another aspect which is the growth of evolutionary ascent. Nothing is lost, that is to say, everything which grows, everything which rises, everything which increases, everything which develops has for counterbalance somewhere something which is consumed, which is burnt.

NOTHING GROWS EXCEPT BY A DEATH,

So many litres of petrol in the car, so many kilometers travelled. This petrol must be burnt, this petrol must be used up, to make the car go. And our world does not function unless somewhere there is something which is burnt up and consumed for the progress of mankind. Nothing progresses, nothing rises, nothing grows unless something suffers or dies for it...

The Lebanese Jesuit Father Henri Ayrouth, who founded the "Association of Schools in Upper Egypt" died some years ago. Do you know what he did? He had been in a hospice and in a hospital and had seen the incurably ill, tied to their bed for years, weak and helpless, and he said to them: "I want to found this new important Association on you, on your suffering, on your helplessness and sadness. Please give it all to me, I need that energy to create something. I need your weakness, that it may become very strong somewhere. I need you." At first they did not understand how they could be of any help, being paralysed sick and old, and Father Ayrouth had to explain it carefully. Then he founded his work on these weak and helpless people in hospital, incapable of moving. And it flourishes still, even after the death of the founder, better than ever! It grows, it develops, because it was consciously founded on the suffering of all these beings, incapable of moving and helping him but able to provide a creative energy, without which every action is sterile.

And I am reminded of the Curé of Ars, Saint Jean-Marie Vianney. The Curé of Ars longed to make conversions, but he was not good in talking, his words were awkward. So he would pass one full night kneeling down in a painful suffering in order to "buy" these souls, as he put it:

"Father, let me buy them!"

By a mortification, by an extraordinary sacrifice, he paid the price for making conversions simply by a few words. But first he had paid, he had "bought" this Spiritual Renaissance which he had wanted to awaken and to rise. Saint Exupery also understood. He said:

"Thou art root of a tree which lives of thee."

For there are in the world people who take action, who do lots of things, who speak up loudly - like me and others. These are the ones you see or hear about, but there are those in secret and known only to God. They pray, they suffer, they offer. And they are the ones who are responsible for the GOOD that can be done. I know that if any charity is done by me, people do not owe it to me but to certain persons I know who offer for me, who pray for me, who suffer for me. I know that, I feel it, and I know that I am only the mouth which speaks and the legs which run, but the energy comes from somewhere else... My work, it is not I who give it - or very little -, it comes from somewhere else, and it is a mystery. "Thou art root of a tree that lives of thee".

Nothing is useless and no-one is useless in this world. The old man, bent by the years and no more able to work, he is perhaps more useful than the man who makes much ado in the market place. And the sick man in his hospital bed, he also takes part. The whole world takes part, we are one. Each of us in his own way takes part and nothing is ever lost.

There is action and there is passion, and passion is perhaps more efficacious than action. Jesus Christ has saved the world not by his action but by his passion at the moment when he acted no more, at the moment when he suffered. It was not at the moment when he spoke that he saved the world, but when he was silent that the great work was done on Good Friday.

Effectiveness is not judged by the words we say but by the gestures we make, by the actions we carry out and by the work which we create. But all this can be very superficial, if there is no soul. Without soul all is nothing, and the soul comes from somewhere, from something which is offered and burnt. Something is consumed that something else can proceed and grow.

I do not know if you have seen the old film *Le Defroque*. There was once a demand to unfrock a priest who had given up his life principles of priesthood. At a certain moment they showed in the film all people who were praying for him: in different convents, in his family, in the houses of his friends to right and to left: "LORD, please open his eyes!" Rather melodramatic perhaps, but never mind, it was very expressive! One saw the priest alone, reflecting and struggling to find his path, one saw the prayers in union around him, which arose for him in a kind of deep collective wish.

And then finally, these prayers became victorious over the rub inside him. All this expresses not suffering exactly, but it expresses the communion of beings beyond the realm of appearances, beyond the visible. There is a communion in the invisible in which we do not believe enough but which is true and even more true than that which we call the visible.

And then there is something which is beyond this life, in the catholic language called Purgatory. It means for me: a man, during his life, has not accomplished a complete and total dispossession of his Self by suffering which is the condition for his self-realisation; but now in the Other Life by purgatory, or whatever you like to call it, he continues his development and further growth. For me, purgatory is a very interesting reality, because no man has completed his spiritual itinerary on this earth, none of us achieves here the full stature of man. There is a path for us to follow and a purification to complete in the Other World. What is the shape of purgatory, what is its face? I do not know, but for me there are in that Other World beings, human souls, who "burn" for us, who furnish our humanity with the energy we lack, so we may continue the process of our growth and finally reach the end of our path.

For me, evolution, this progress in life, this ascent, this growth, is possible only by the mystery of suffering and death. If there were not an engine inside called suffering and death, there would be no ascent, no growth, there would be no evolution. The universe rises because there is a totalisation in death which provides the evolutionary process with its ascentional dynamism.

but what is in question is for us to live suffering in this perspective. In other words, the suffering, which sooner or later we all must face and which we have all, more or less, known, instead of living it as a destiny or a fatality which bears down on us, against us in spite of us, we must accept it with faith and make of it an offering an obligation, a sacrifice, an act of freedom and a creative act.

Transform your destiny into a free choice, transform your suffering into a creative birth, and in this way give it its meaning.

(Ref E)

The aspects of healing: Illness is a state of being, when the person is not completely possessed by the Spirit. This is why we not only have psychosomatic medicine, but I believe in pneuma-psychosomatic medicine. Nowadays, medicine has developed worldwide into psychosomatic medicine, because they have found that the roots of many diseases are in the psyche, not only in the body. This is a step in the right direction, but not the last step. I believe that the pneuma is deeper than the psyche. And as long as you do not reach that level, you cannot heal the body.

And this is why, when they lowered the paralysed man down from the roof in front of Jesus, he did not heal his body before healing his soul and the Spirit. He said: "Your sins are forgiven". And silently, the man said to himself: I did not come in order that my sins be forgiven, I came in order that my legs be healed! Jesus replied: "Did you know that the cause of this man's illness was spiritual?" Therefore, I think that medicine should comprise the third dimension, which is called the pneumatic or the spiritual dimension. This was the tendency of Viktor Frankl, Karl Rogers, Erich Fromm. There you have the tendency to introduce the spiritual elements when curing people. And this is why I am a priest and not a psychiatrist. C.G. Jung was the first to start this idea.

(Ref D)

We tend to believe that death is a future state into which we will enter one day when we have finished our existence. This is false, Death is not a future state. It is a present state, a zone of our being. Until we have grasped that, I think we do not understand death at all. We put it at the end of a journey, as if it came at the end of life, while it is not the end of life, but the heart of it. As long as death is not lived in the present, we do not know what it is and we will never meet it, because true death is lived in the present, here, now. It is in me. It is a zone of my being to be crossed. If I cross it, I am already in eternity, I am in the beyond, I have already risen, I am already in God. I am already in eternal life.

If, on the other hand, I have not crossed it, even if I die a physical death, I am not yet on the other side. To die physically is not dying. The only death which a human being can die is that which he dies in his freedom, in his inner being. We die in our freedom before we die in our bodies. If this act is not accomplished, our death will have to begin again. In a small way it is what is called purgatory. Purgatory would be this death beyond death by which the human being gains access to eternal life. One further remark: although we can talk at length about this matter, my aim is not to talk about death, because death and resurrection go together, they are the same act. On the one hand it is called death, on the other hand it is called resurrection, but it is the same reality. When I die, I rise, and when I rise it is in the very act of dying that I rise.

(Ref H)

My vision is that in daily life there is always hope, an issue, an outlet for every situation which seems hopeless. Is there anything more hopeless than death? Death is the end of everything. But our Christian faith tells us it could be a new beginning. This is the challenge of faith. It is not enough to be optimistic, thanks to one's genes or hormones. Optimism has to be based on faith and confidence. It means surmounting pessimism. My optimism is not primary optimism where everything is ok, or not ok. I know that there are all kinds of evil around me and in me! But the optimism of a believing Christian is one of hope, a Paschal hope. What do I mean by Paschal hope? A hope beyond death! When a situation is hopeless, for example a death, just consider that faith can revive dead people! Read about the resurrection of Lazarus in St. John. Lazarus had been dead for four days! His sister Martha believes in Jesus, she has hope. And Jesus says to her:

"I am the resurrection,
if anyone believes in me,
even though he dies he will live, and
whoever lives and believes in me, will never die.
Do you believe this?

(John 11, 26)

Yes! The Gospel is a message beyond death, beyond human hope. This is what I try to live in my daily life. There is no hopeless situation, there is always something BEYOND.

(Ref O)

Since our childhood we have been told that when we die we will go to heaven if we have lived in the right way. Jesus said "I have prepared rooms and lodgings for you in heaven, do not be afraid" What does this mean if Jesus is still on earth?

Imagine yourself in heaven, enjoying being there, and

people suffering so many dramas on earth. Would you be happy? Could you accept being in heaven when your friends and relatives are not there? It's simply impossible! We have to rethink what heaven is and where it is. Heaven is here. People who die are not taken away like Jesus on the Ascension pictures of our artists, no, they continue their journey with their loved ones. Those who die do not go away, they continue their journey with us, in us, through us until, all together, we will reach heaven. This is a happier conception of heaven. Heaven will be for everybody or for nobody. I dislike the idea of a heaven which is only for some, no thank you! Because heaven is love, and Jesus is Emmanuel, and he will be with all of us.

(Ref S)

THE CONCRETE WALL

cf. The parable of the rich man and Lazarus

(Luke16, 19-31)

In these days Jesus and his friends, engrossed in conversation, passed by a large five-star hotel in town. "Follow me!" Jesus said suddenly and, striding across the well cared-for lawns to the hotel entrance, walked over to the reception desk. He was interested in the prices: single room with bath - $150, luxury suite - $800. And up above the price-list a notice saying "No vacancies!"

Everyone knew what the thick concrete wall out there hid from the hotel guests' eyes: a huge cancerous tumour which grew ever bigger and spread endlessly - the slums. But the wall did not stop hundreds of skinny children, barefoot and in rags, from darting to and fro. They prowled round the hotel buildings scrounging for something to eat and begged surreptitiously when the staffs backs were turned. The tourists refused to take any notice of these children, as they were repugnant to look at and disturbed the otherwise pleasant surroundings.

Day after day these half-starved children, their eyes wide-open, stared through the dining-hall windows, reveling in the sight of the over-abundance of delicacies within. What happened to those countless untouched dishes which were continuously taken back to the kitchen. It would seem that the foreign guests preferred to chat, laugh or even doze off, rather than enjoy their food. Strange. Could anyone understand that?

Then the children tore themselves away from this vision of "the land of milk and honey" and, in order to forget it, began to play football on the immaculate lawns with a "ball" they had made out of rags. Their game, however, was short-lived for hardly had they began, when two hotel employees, in gold-embroidered livery, hastened over and, showering swear-words at the intruders and told them to go to hell.

Jesus went after one of the poor youngsters to ask him a few questions:

"Tell me, how are things at home? Has your Dad got a job?"

"He gets by."

"Do you know how much he manages to earn in a month?"

"About a hundred pounds."

"And your Mum?"

"She has to stay home as I have four younger brothers and sisters."

"What's your flat like?"

"Flat...? We've only got one room and one bed in the basement of a small house."

"And a toilet?"

"There isn't one. And no water either. Our Mum fetches it from the

communal pump in the area."

The boy then ran off and disappeared behind the wall.

Jesus was beside himself. He bit his lip hard in order not to explode with fury. Then he said to one of the friends accompanying him:

"The father of that child earns one hundred pounds a month, that is thirty dollars. If my calculations are correct, then a guest in this luxurious hotel squanders this family's entire two-years' income in one single night! That is quite beyond comprehension! How can one accept that a gulf of this dimension should separate these two worlds from one another?"

"Have you read the latest UNDP report?" one of his friends asked him, referring to a UN development programme report. "There the division is shown in a more general perspective, namely between the rich and poor countries, even those within the same region, as for instance, the Arab countries to which we belong. Thus the average annual income per head in the United Arab Emirates is $15,000 while in Somalia it is a mere$150. The difference is 1:100 and compared to the countries these tourists come from, it is certainly even greater. Say something, Jesus, please!"

Controlling his anger, Jesus quietly reminded his friends of his own words spoken long ago:

"But alas for you who are rich: You are having your consolation now." (Luke 6, 24) If I thereby cursed the rich, then certainly not because they were rich, as wealth in itself is not a curse. On the contrary, money and property can become a blessing, if one learns to share. They can make a man great, wonderfully great! In most cases, however, prosperity shuts doors and isolates the rich. It cuts them off and makes them blind, deaf and indifferent towards the needs of their fellowmen. That is the curse of personal wealth. No, the curse is not on money or possessions, but on the selfishness which results from it and which makes people so terribly callous and thick-skinned and finally turns them into stone.

Look at these tourists! They rush from one sightseeing "must" to the next and take in every museum and place of fame in their country. And by doing so they exhaust valuable energy and make themselves sick with gourmet food. And not one of them would ever want to venture even a few steps behind this concrete wall to discover the naked truth about a slum area in our present world.

For this wall, dear friends, is surely symbolic of that other wall which stands upright in their hearts. It is a sign that they have closed the door, possibly forever. The unbridgeable gulf I talked of that time in the parable of the rich man and Lazarus, remember? (Luke 16, 19-32) is the gulf between heaven and hell. It is a sign that a hardened heart, which has retreated into its shell and become cold, is incapable of bridging the gap which separates it from other human hearts. In reality the rich of this world have erected that concrete wall over there in the centre of their own hearts, and they have dug the gulf which separates them from the poor with their own hands and made it so deep and wide that they can no longer cross it.

Why....? No Power in the world, not even Almighty God, can force free human being who refuse to love their neighbours to open their hearts. People who are wrapped up in themselves, who have only themselves in mind will remain prisioners of their own egos, lonely and isolated forever.

Now do you understand what is meant by the term "hell"?" His friends were shaken. "Yes," they replied, "we have understood"

And the group continued on their way through the town.

(Ref L)

Chapter 5:
The State of Prayer

The state of prayer is a state of total relaxation and abandonment. In this state of "letting go", God can express himself and inspire the soul. For many people, prayer means saying prayers. If you fill the time of prayer with saying prayers, God cannot speak to you. Prayer means offering to God an empty soul, an empty mind, a blank sheet of paper on which He can write. One of the most important elements of prayer, especially of mystical prayer, is to create a void within yourself, not to fill it up with words and ideas. Let the Spirit be free within you!

There is a very meaningful story in Nikos Kazantzakis' famous novel *Christ recrucified*. A monk named Manolis is seen to open his eyes in front of a wonderful landscape, and then close them very quickly again. One of his fellow monks asks him: "*Why do you close your eyes? You must open them to contemplate God's wonderful creation!*" He answers:

"I open my eyes in order to contemplate creation, then I close them in order to contemplate the creator."

The exterior senses often prevent us from entering deeper. We need to close our eyes and our ears, we need to fast and abstain from touching things in order to develop the deeper feelings of our soul. Our age is an age of over-stimulation of our senses. We feel agitated by pictures, films, television, all kinds of powerful exterior stimuli! I was having dinner with a Carmelite Father in a kind of disco. There were booming loudspeakers and a flood of lights everywhere! Well, they have these in Prague just as we have them in Cairo, Alexandria, and all over the world. It is a new youth culture, but a kind of continuous irritation of the senses until you are unable to experience anything essential because there is an excess of everything.

Sometimes I see people walking in the countryside with a walkman and earphones. They escape from the city but they take the city with them; they escape from the noise but they take it with them! Instead of enjoying the peace and silence of the countryside they bring city life with them. Finally they become incapable of real listening and understanding. Hearing presupposes a background of silence from which the melody of the song detaches itself and emerges in all its purity. The same process takes place with a work of art, a painting. If everything is clear, nothing will appear. Light cannot appear unless there is a background of darkness. Mysticism teaches us: what we are lacking today is a kind of darkness, a night that delivers a message. There is no night in our cities any more, no night in our lives. We use neon, spots and streetlights and make night into day. This excess of electricity has killed the sense of darkness in us. What is nice about daytime is that it follows the long night; what is nice about spring is that it follows the long winter. But we refuse darkness, we refuse winter. Modern Man needs continuous stimulation and strong feelings, and forgets a period of void, an emptiness, in between.

This means that nowadays we need a kind of asceticism, an absence of something. Asceticism means lacking something in order to experience life more intensely. You cannot appreciate the goodness of fresh water unless you have already experienced thirst. I remember going on an excursion with some 13 year-old boys in the desert around Cairo. The temperature was about 42° in the shade. We walked under the sun for hours and hours. Our water bottles were empty and we were looking for some fresh water. Never in my life have I felt such thirst, my body was dry as a stone. All of a sudden we discovered a little house which had a tap. We threw ourselves down on the ground, turned on the tap and started drinking hastily.

Experiencing the absence of something is essential in order to realize the value of it. The same happens with a person who has enjoyed good health all his life and who suddenly breaks down and is obliged to stay in bed for some months. When he recovers and can walk again, he realizes for the first time what it means to be able to walk and be carried by one's own two legs. To understand something is to accept not understanding it for a time. In order to experience something we have to accept not experiencing it for a while. If you want to experience fine music, don't listen to music all day long. If you want to experience light, try to experience darkness beforehand. If you want to experience movement, keep still for a while.

(Ref M)

There are many techniques of prayer including that in which you recapitulate the past day in the light of God. The means are not important. What is important is whether or not the means bring you to prayer. All the means are good but not the same for everyone. Each person has, at different times, a specific way which can help him pray. On certain days I like to pray in Church, on other days I want to pray in the underground, or while walking in nature, on some days I use physical attitudes, on other days I experience an obstacle to prayer which I accept. At one point I was practising Yoga exercises, legs crossed and so on, but when I discovered that they were an obstacle to prayer I dropped them. Sometimes I use vocal prayers like the Rosary and the Psalms. I feel completely free about the means I use. The founder of the Jesuit Order, St. Ignatius of Loyola writes in his *Spiritual Exercises* that you must adopt the means of prayer which helps you most in reaching your aim: standing, kneeling, lying down, or walking, whatever you want. Everyone has to search for the means most helpful towards good prayer. This is often in contradiction with the physical attitudes which some Guru has imposed on his disciples as a must, kind of law! Those are certainly not the ways of the Spirit!

(Ref M)

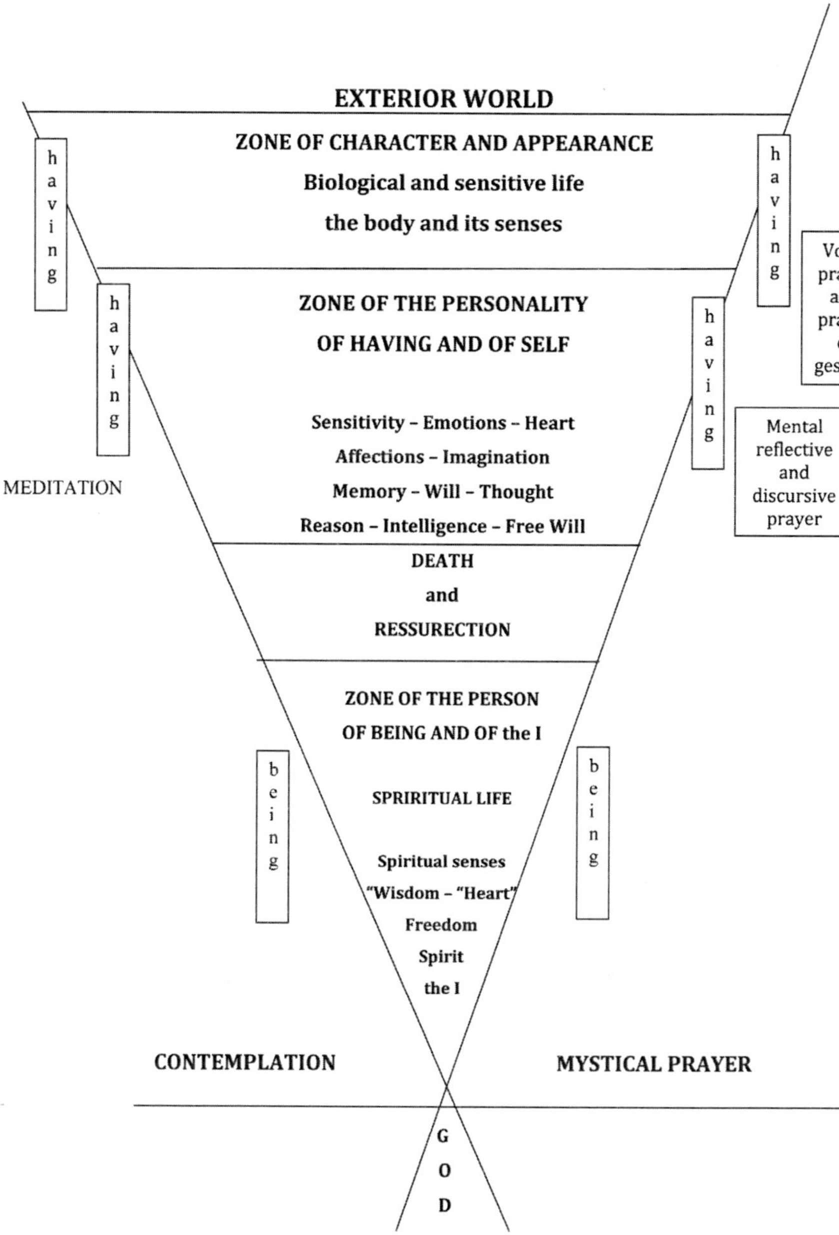
EXTERIOR WORLD
ZONE OF CHARACTER AND APPEARANCE
Biological and sensitive life
the body and its senses
having
having
Vocal prayer and prayer of gesture
ZONE OF THE PERSONALITY
OF HAVING AND OF SELF
Sensitivity – Emotions – Heart
Affections – Imagination
Memory – Will – Thought
Reason – Intelligence – Free Will
having
having
MEDITATION
Mental reflective and discursive prayer
DEATH
and
RESSURECTION
ZONE OF THE PERSON
OF BEING AND OF the I
SPRIRITUAL LIFE
Spiritual senses
"Wisdom – "Heart"
Freedom
Spirit
the I
being
being
CONTEMPLATION
MYSTICAL PRAYER
G
O
D

Starting with this diagram, I am now going to situate prayer and prayers. Here you have verbal prayer and prayer of gesture which are at the level of the body. I say words, I gesture; liturgy for example is at this level. This does not mean that it is only at this level, for verbal prayer and prayer of gesture can carry a mystical dimension, but in as much as it is verbal prayer and prayer of gesture, it is situated at the level of the body.

Take a second type of prayer which is mental prayer, reflective and discursive prayer. This is meditation. The word meditation is ambiguous, because sometimes we say that we meditate, meaning that we are saying our prayers. To be precise, I think we ought to reserve the word "meditation" for mental, reflective and discursive prayer. It is prayer which follows a chain of ideas in a logical and rational way. This prayer is not yet prayer, it is a way forward.

Real prayer is at the point of the cone. Here we have the peak, the aim, mystical prayer or contemplation, which is meeting God, dialogue, intimate conversation. All the rest is a means. In quick succession, we have situated the three essential forms of prayer in the diagram of the personality. Now, using the outline, I would like to reflect on the process of prayer with you.

St. Ignatius of Loyola has a very simple diagram for prayer. Some of you will even find it simplistic. However, it contains very great wisdom. In this diagram, I want to stress only two points - the point of departure and the point of arrival. St. Ignatius says: you must pray with the act of the presence of God, then follow the application of the senses, of the intelligence, of the emotions and finally of dialogue. Have we reflected what this departure point represents, and this point of arrival? It means that prayer begins with our presence before God. And ends with a meeting with God.

It moves from the departure point to the point of arrival and joins the departure point by means of the point of arrival. All the rest is to be found between the two points, and prayer is also sandwiched between the departure point, which is the presence of God, and the point of arrival which is dialogue with God, which means that the main point in prayer is meeting God. And not reflecting on God.

It is very enlightening to think about that. All the rest fits into the middle. If there is "that at the beginning" and "that at the end", all the rest is prayer also.

If I start to pray, I take a spiritual book and read fifteen pages during my half-hour of meditation, it's good work. Then I put the book down. I haven't prayed. I've reflected on God, I've read interesting things, I've even taken notes, but I haven't prayed. I've meditated perhaps, but I haven't prayed.

Another way of expressing it would be – the first image is the sandwich I spoke about earlier, the second image is the circle. This image of the circle is interesting, because when you draw a circle you begin with a point and you finish where you began. So the point of arrival joins up with the point of departure in a circle – this is very important. In other words, in prayer there is a procedure: I must start where I want to arrive, and I must arrive where I left off. If I cannot start with the presence of God, well, I will never arrive at the presence of God. Communication will not take place. The image of the circle is very important because it indicates something else as well. It shows me that if I have established a good starting point, a good presence of God at the beginning, and if I try to close the circle through dialogue, I may not finish my hour of meditation, the interior of the circle is of little importance.

In concrete terms - listen carefully because I think it is very important - when I have made this circle which begins with God and finishes with God, what I put inside is of no importance. Whether I think of the bell, whether I think about my glasses, whether I think of my slippers, whether I think of tomorrow's work, whether I think about a problem I have, whether I think of the quarrel I had, whether I think about that business I have to do, these are not distractions. The word distraction in prayer is a very ambiguous word, and many people spend their time getting rid of distractions instead of simply giving themselves up to God because once you are in the circle there are no distractions, everything is prayer.

Let me explain, using two lovers as an example. When two people are in love, it does not matter what they talk about - the rain, the weather, a passing train, cooking, what they drink. Whether they say little or a lot, whether they talk about St. Thomas Aquinas, or about what they eat, hasn't the slightest importance. All that is love. It is not even the content of what they say that counts. What counts is the climate in which they are, the rest is only a means.

In prayer, we must not worry as long as these distractions happen in the circle. If they are in the circle, they are not distractions. If there is no circle, then thinking about God or Our Lady or St. Rita or all the saints in heaven will be distractions, it won't be prayer. So, of the two possibilities, either we are in the circle and all the profane in the circle is prayer, or else the circle has not been formed, and all the holiness which is not in the circle, all the holiness which you could have stored in the depth of yourself is not prayer. What makes prayer meaningful is not the content of what you say, or what you have in your heart, but the climate in which you bathe. The content is of little importance. Whether you read St. John of the Cross, the Bible or the finest book on spirituality (because the content is beyond words, or the reality that you live is beyond words), is not very important.

Here is another explanation: no matter what you do, your spirit works. You will never be able to stop it, and your imagination works like the cinema all the time. You will never be able to stop it, never. Consequently, don't make any effort to banish your distractions or your images, or try to resist them. It works on its own. That's how it is. Living is seeing your spirit think; living is seeing your imagination function; living is seeing your heart become attached. That's how it is. So don't fight against it. Orientate all that in a definite direction. Put yourself in a particular climate and all that is prayer.

Praying is very simple. It means "playing" in a circle. Playing, playing! Playing is very important. Prayer which is not playing is boring prayer, both for you and for God. God loves to play with you, so, once we have done all that, he says "Play, give yourself up, let yourself go, think about what you like, you are in my arms, in the arms of your Father". If you like let the circle be the two arms of God and you are in God's bosom. That's the way it is. You are in him, he has taken you over. There he says to you "Play like a child; give yourself up." The game has no constraints, the game is free, the game is coming and going. I have no aim in my prayer. I don't aim to ask for a cure for my friend, or for success in my exams. I'm not looking for anything. To want something in prayer is to see your prayer fail and that is why the great enemy of prayer is will. You mustn't want anything. Entering into prayer is not an act of will. Once you are into prayer, will plays no further role.

Prayer itself is pure spontaneity, but only on condition that you are present, that you have crossed this zone. If you haven't crossed it, then yes, distractions exist, all the rest exists. But once you are there, once you have crossed that, nothing can separate us from the love of Christ, from the love of God in Jesus, our Saviour. As St Paul writes: Neither life nor death, nor the past or present, can separate us from God because we are beyond life and death, beyond the past and present. We are in eternity; nor can the heights or depths separate us from God because we are beyond the heights and the depths. We are in the zone where - everything is over - we can no longer escape God. We are in his arms, we are caught and we surrender.

My first image was that of a sandwich. My second image was that of a circle. I will now use a third image for the same reality which I am talking about, and which is that of presence in emptiness and presence in fullness.

Let me explain. When I begin to pray, I make an act of the presence of God in emptiness. When I finish praying, I find the act of the presence of God in full. The emptiness has been filled. What we find at the very beginning of prayer in emptiness, in the form of a search, a desire, we will find at the end of prayer in full, in the form of fullness, of an encounter. So we cannot say that the beginning of prayer is like the end of prayer. This is not the case, it is different. But there is a kind of emptiness afterwards which is a call, a cry, a desire, a thirst, a hunger, a waiting. All these words meet to say: I am an emptiness which is waiting to be filled. If there is not this emptiness, if there is not this hollowness, God cannot come. There is nothing for him to fill. If I pour litres of water onto a table, the table will not fill up because it is flat. For the table to fill up it must be hollow. If the heart is like a table, God will come and he will spread himself in me but I will retain nothing because it will slip and fall. The fullness of God can only reach me and fill me if I become "capacity" - which means longing and waiting.

Prayer must be situated at the level of dialogue, of intimate conversation if it is to meet up with itself at the same level. As long as we are not at that point, we are not in prayer.

This is very important because many people who don't pray think they pray, and many who think they don't pray, do. For many people, praying is saying prayers. For many people praying is meditating, but they do not pray because they are outside this essential dialogue. For others who live a mystical, a truly mystical dimension to their lives, which contains neither verbal nor mental prayer, they are truly at prayer. That is the first point. A more philosophical way of saying it would be this: prayer develops in three stages:

- a stage of posing - a stage of opposing - a stage of going beyond.

So we have thesis, antithesis, synthesis. I pose, I oppose, I sublimate. But what does that mean in prayer? In prayer, first I make the act of presence of God which is posing. When I have taken this step, I have taken the negative way. This negative way is the most important as a way. All three are important, but the mystics insist a lot on the negative way in between. The negative way consists of purifying the idea of God of all errors, of all that which is not God.

Who is God? That is the question. From that moment I tend to make a representation of him. I say to myself: "I am making an act of the presence of God. God is beside me. He is looking at me. He sees me. He hears me." We need this representation of God in order to imagine God. The way of negation I am speaking about, comes in here to correct every representation of God. Every representation of God is an idol, and the negative way is there in order to stop us falling into idolatry.

This is essential because man always has the tendency to make an image of God for himself, either an image of stone, or a golden calf, a picture or poetry formed in the imagination. Then we can imagine God. But God is still beyond the grasp of the imagination. God is beyond the senses. You cannot put your hand on God. You cannot measure Him or go around Him. Because what is an idol? An idol is the possibility of going around God. An idol is the possibility of having power over God. An idol is the possibility of having God before us, of possessing Him, of looking at Him, of touching Him, of taking possession of Him. It's your hand. ," Israel, this is your God who brought you out of the land of Egypt." That is what the Jews said about the golden calf. Every image of God is idolatry of the same type, because it is precisely a representation which represents nothing, a representation which is not representative, the first commandment of God "you will have no other God but me".

This is the way it is. In this negative way there is always a second purification, the first being that of the senses and of the imagination. The second is that of intelligence and of reason, because in the same way as we can wish to represent God physically or mentally, in the same way we can wish to represent him at the level of intelligence, make an idea of God and not an image of God. This is still idolatry. Idolatry, not of the senses and the imagination but of the intelligence, because intelligence also has its idols. And after a certain amount of time reflecting on God, intelligent people think they have understood God, whom they have shut up in their minds, in their concepts.

God has become the prisoner of an intellectual framework. The second type of idolatry is that of the intelligence. Trying to understand God is as serious as trying to take hold of Him. Taking and understanding (prendre, comprendre) have the same root, one at the level of the senses - the hand which takes - the other at the level of the intelligence the brain which takes hold of God. In both cases it is not God. It is an idol. In both cases we are dealing with an idol. This is why prayer must pass through the first night of the senses, as St. John of the Cross says, and through the second night, the night of the intelligence, of reason, of the spirit, which brings a second purification.

You can see how, we are joining the great ways of John of the Cross in prayer. Idolatry being the great sin of man, we can do so in prayer, which we consider as the most sacred, most religious act, but fall into paganism, wishing to possess God.

There is a third way of possessing him - it's through the heart and the emotions. And there too the negative way also purifies this zone. We can still wish to possess God. "My little Jesus", "My God", "You and I are fine together", so we keep God, we lock him in our hearts, it is the same attempt again, this greed for God. "I have tasted God in my heart, I have felt him". Then you want to try to keep him with all sorts of little tricks so that this feeling you have tasted won't go away - this presence, this sweetness! Man's temptation is to say to himself: "I'll keep it, I'll savour it" There is your spiritual greed at an emotional level. The three positions - of the senses, of the imagination and the intelligence and of the heart, are all three of the same type: the spirit of possessing God. But prayer is poverty and humility.

You haven't reached God until you have understood that. You can't put your hands on God. You can't shut God in. You cannot possess God. It is He who puts His hands on you.

"You put your hand on me." (Ps. 139)

It is He who loves us and not we who love Him. We are loved by Him, and it is the act of decentralization of prayer where we no longer love God, but let ourselves be loved by God, and then comes the big change-over which takes place in ourselves, to live prayer on a real level. At that moment we enter into the third zone of prayer. After this triple purification: senses, imagination and intelligence, emotions, we enter into God. God, He who changes my very name. "What is your name?" Jacob asks God. "I will not tell you my name. But now you will be called Israel." Everything changes the moment we receive our new name from God, the one which one day we will be given on a little white stone at the end of the race. It is no longer we who discover the name of God, it is God who gives us our final name. There can be a fundamental change-over in prayer, we are completely changed.

Now we find ourselves by losing ourselves. We fall into God's orbit. It is as if the rocket takes off slowly, rises above the earth, and then suddenly falls into the moon's orbit, different from ours. In prayer, there is a moment when we lose balance and we fall into God's orbit. It is this act of losing balance which is the essential in prayer, otherwise we will never fall into God, and every possession, every greed, every spirit of riches, is exactly the act which kills prayer.

I am not going to talk about the third stage because it goes too far and it is too personal. I think you have understood a little with this diagram what I experience. At the end of this process, man finds what he has left, all that he lost, all that he sacrificed, he regains it but on a spiritual level. He who wants to save his life, loses it, and he who loses it, finds it again says Jesus. We find ourselves again, and we find all we left, and all we lost, once we have crossed over the threshold, Everything is given back to us a hundredfold.

This is an extraordinary experience, where emotion joins spirit, and intelligence joins spirit. At that moment we have our senses, and at the spiritual level we touch, at the spiritual level we see, we taste, we feel, all that is true. It is tangible but it is also spiritual. It is here that the two meet; there is no opposition. There is opposition only for he who has not taken the step, but for he who has, there is no opposition.

It is the zone of reconciliation with oneself. Finally a being is reconciled with his body, with his intelligence. Everything which we renounced, which we refused in a certain way, which we sacrificed freely, we find at the level of wisdom. All becomes one, heart and emotion and intelligence are one single act. We understand with our hearts.

Finally, the free will which I sacrificed in the act of obedience, I find again in the freedom of the children of God. Freedom is even beyond choice. You can no longer choose. I am beyond choice. Freedom is fixed in God, just as the saint in heaven is fixed in God, freedom which can no longer choose because it is fixed in the good, because it is fixed in love, because it is fixed in God. And that is the zone of the spirit, of spiritual life. Man reaches himself, purifies himself. It is the total union with himself, in reconciliation, in unity.

(Ref H)

Any action not rooted in prayer is an empty action. Any action which does not stem from a deep personal experience of God is simply nothing. For me, prayer is the soul of action. Action stems from being. Acting can mean changing nothing, you change by what you ARE, but not by what you DO. Being is the most essential thing, and then action follows like a manifestation, an exteriorisation of what you feel innermost, of what you are. Prayer is not only said in Church or at home, prayer is being at one with God. Then, when you act, it is not you, it is God acting within you, through you, with you; it is not only your action, it's also God's action.

(Ref J)

That is what prayer is. That is why prayer is the most important act of the human being, the act by which man meets himself, rejoins his origin, finds himself, and finds God and finding God, finds himself.

When we say “prayer”, most people don’t understand. But they understand a lot of other things, a lot of very boring things.

(Ref H)

THE FULLNESS OF LIFE

Jesus, You came to give us
the fullness of life
and you said:
"I have come so that they may have life
and have it to the full" (John 10, 10b)
I would like to take this invitation
very seriously today.
I would like to understand that my life can never be repeated.
What I have lived today
is gained forever,
what I have not lived today
is lost forever.
Grant me the sense of my responsibility,
to give all that I can give today,
to love whom I can love today,
and to find thereby the deepest joy
of loving and giving and being,
by following you in your path
which is the path of Truth.
In becoming myself
I will become Everything in You.

(Ref K)

Chapter 6: The Purpose of the Eucharist

What is love? Everyone knows; no one knows. We have never finished discovering and knowing what love is. For Teilhard de Chardin, love is the universal force of union which pushes the elements of the cosmos together, so that they join up. Love is a universal force at work from the very beginning of time. Love is the energy that causes atoms to unite to form molecules, which combine to form mega molecules and then cells and multi-cellular substances, which are increasingly complex. Love is the energy that pushes a man towards a woman and a woman to a man and the two towards their child and the child to its parents.

This idea of love and of unity in the world and in nature is only achieved through us. We have as our vocation to accomplish this dream inherent in the world. In other words this world dream will only be achieved through man, and this will only be brought about through the world. There is between man and the world a complementary and reciprocal movement.

This progression in nature is seen in the Eucharist. What is this bread and wine of the Eucharist? It is the earth that has been worked, ploughed and turned over. It is the seed that has accepted death in order to give life. It is water that has accepted to flow in the clay in order to allow it to germinate. It is the sun that has communicated its energy and which slowly allows the seed to grow. It is the air around the plant that gives it oxygen. Thus is formed the ear of grain.

Man takes the ear and begins his work of turning the soil and irrigating it and finally harvesting it. Taking it then to the mill and eventually to the bakery.

Finally the bread arrives on the altar. Are we aware that this bread is the coming together of a great movement which goes from the sun to the earth, to the river, the sea, the air, the wind, all that and then the work of man, "fruit of the earth and work of man"? Moreover, when we hear that phrase at Mass, we automatically say, "Blessed be God now and for ever" We should say, "It is fantastic." What the priest holds up is the immense work of creation of which St Paul speaks: "The whole of creation is in labour", yes it is the work of all who have collaborated in order that this bread becomes possible, becomes someone, becomes the Body of Christ. There is here an extraordinary mystery. In the Eucharist, nature takes on a face, it becomes someone!............

I will now pose the following question: the molecule sacrifices itself for the small plant, the plant sacrifices itself for the sheep, the sheep for the child and the child, to whom is he to be sacrificed? What is the highest reality to which he must give himself? Take me, eat me! In opening the Gospel we read: "Take and eat, this is my body. Take and drink, this is my blood" "He who eats me will live by me", "He who eats the flesh of the Son of Man and drinks his blood has eternal life". There is a connection here: "Take me up from the earth so that I become a small blade of grass" "Take me from the soil so that I become a little white sheep. Take me, eat me...." But then how is it that it is not I who say, "O Christ, take and eat, this is my body"? But it is he who says it?

Strange! The role is reversed. It is the contrary that occurs. This is striking, it should be the man who says to Christ: "Take me, eat me, so that I become your body" whereas it is the reverse that occurs. When I go to

Communion, it is not Christ who enters into me, it is I who enter into him, into his Body, his mystical Body. The Eucharist is the last stage in evolution by which man, being assimilated into the world and the cosmos, is himself assimilated in his turn by the one who gives him access to the world and the cosmos in its full dimension.

The end of the world will come when the material world has been taken on, assumed by Man, when the various energies of the cosmos will have been transformed into energy radiating from the centre,that is spiritualised. But this will still not be the end, because it will be necessary that Man, humanity, in its turn, offers itself to be divinised. The last stage of evolution is the stage of oblation or offering, in which humanity allows itself to be taken, offered in a gesture of abandonment in which the world is raised up and divinised. This is what Teilhard de Chardin calls "Christification".

The Eucharist represents and expresses this stage: sacrifice. God makes himself our food so that we can become his food. He enters into us so that we can enter into him. Everything happens under the form of eating and drinking, the meal. The meal has always been seen by people as a sacrifice. Sacrifice and meal go together since antiquities.

Recently I met Karim, one of the parishioners in our Jesuit church in Alexandria and also one of my pupils whom I had known since a child. he is now 40 years old and has a young son of six years, named Mourad. Karim said to me: "Father Boulad, Mourad asks me questions I'm unable to answer" This good Karim had followed courses on the catechism and studied many authors of theology, but didn't know how to reply to his son. He asked me to help him. I told him "Bring the boy here". I then invited the youngster to sit down and asked him what he wanted to know. He replied, "Is it really Jesus present in the host, in the bread and the wine? Is it him?" How could I answer him? I improvised, and asked Karim, the father, to get a photo of himself. He brought it and I said to the boy, "whose photo is this?" "It's a photo of Daddy" answered Mourad. "Does Daddy travel often?" I asked. "Yes". "Before leaving for Cairo, Daddy leaves this photo for you and says to you: Mourad, every time you see this photo, you will know that I am with you?" "Yes" "Are you going to kiss the photo each morning?" "Yes" "And each evening?" "Yes" "But what you're kissing is a piece of paper" "No, it's Daddy" "But no, it's coloured paper" "No, it's Daddy!" Then I go on to reply: "You see, Jesus left on a journey. But before leaving he asked himself how to make us understand that he would remain with us until the end of time. As there were no photos at that time, no canvases, no videos or computers, he said: I'm going to take some bread. he took it and said "this is my body, this is my blood, it's me! You understand?" "Yes, I understand" – He added: every time you do this, I will be with you, every day" – "Ah, yes!"- "What you see, it's what?" – "It's bread" – "Is it bread? No, it's Jesus. What you kiss, is it paper? No it's Daddy.

But that's not all. There is more. Jesus is not like Daddy, he is God. Daddy is a man. But God has said: not only will it be as if I am with you – because this photo is not Daddy in his flesh and bones, it's Daddy who is in Cairo – but Jesus has underlined: I'm going to do more. He is God, he is capable of it. He has said: " It will be me, me truly present. You see bread, but you know that beyond this bread, it's he who is there".

Thus how one can speak to a six-year old, how Jesus is present in the Eucharist. We must invent for each of the mysteries of our earth, which seem so complicated in our Christianity, a story such as the above so that it becomes clearer. I often say that he who knows how to speak to children knows how to speak to the learned. The truth must be so clear to me, so certain, so evident that I can find the language suitable for a child, a learned person, or someone in between. It is for this reason that I often insist on repeating that we need imagination, we need to invent a new language, find a new way of expressing ourselves, of describing those mysteries which are too complicated for most people, but which are for those who have penetrated them, burning with human and divine warmth and truth.

The Eucharist is the prolongation of the Incarnation, its extension in space and time, God with us, Emmanuel, until the end of time. It is the announcement of what is yet to come: "You will do this until I come, until what I have expressed there is realised in truth and fullness"

(Ref X)

Chapter 7: Living life to the Full: Faith and Trust

We have all heard of entropy. Entropy is the devaluation of energy, the loss of energy during the development of our world. If the world is taken by this movement of entropy we all will end in non-being, in emptiness, in void. But Teilhard de Chardin has pointed out that parallel to this movement of entropy there is another movement, an opposite movement, which aims upwards not downwards. He calls it double movement of tangential energy and radial energy, both opposite to each other. And man is the one through whom radial energy is reversing the process.

I'll give you two examples: you have electricity here in this conference, it is energy-consuming. This energy is lost, lost at the material level. But thanks to this light, something is happening in our minds, in our hearts, in our beings, which is growing: consciousness! Through knowledge, through love, through humanity, the loss of energy at the material level is compensated by a growing energy at the spiritual level. What did you eat for lunch? Macaroni, meat, a salad? This is now in your body, it is being destroyed and transformed and raised up to a level of mind, of human energy. So, salad is not salad, it is mind; macaroni is not macaroni, it's thought; a piece of meat is not meat, it's thinking and feeling.

In becoming more and more fully human, we reverse the process of evolution, of entropy and we save the most precious richness of the cosmos. To understand this process is to find a sense and significance to one's personal life. Modern man is living a kind of inner emptiness because he does not understand why he exists. "I exist, but why and for what?" This is a kind of dissolved personality. The emptiness which we now find mainly in developed countries is something tragic. If you don't find a meaning to your existence, your life loses everything. You don't enjoy living, and this is why, in most developed countries, the suicide rate is so high. This is why it is imperative to deliver a message of meaning, of hope, of sense to the new generation and to each of us. Your life has sense, your life has meaning. This meaning is not given before one's commitment and action. Some people think that they first have to decide and clarify a meaning and then go into action, go into commitment. It is in action, through action; by action that I find a meaning. The action has to be done and meaning thereby achieved.

How do you learn to swim? By swimming! How do you learn to live? By living! This is why life supposed a kind of upsurge of the human being in order to say: I'm not giving up! This upsurge is what Paul Tillich calls courage. Life demands courage. You always have to go beyond the stage in which you are. Never abandoning yourself, not letting yourself go! It's easy to give up and say: For what? Why? There's no meaning to life. But we're called every day, when we get up in the morning to get up for something! This movement, this getting up means an act of personal freedom, an act of commitment to life.

For example, sport: jogging, climbing, running, jumping, cycling, swimming. In this sporting action of the body you have a refusal of death, a refusal to let go. I speak about sport because there are so many young people here tonight in this conference hall and they probably indulge in sport. This goes for every human undertaking. For instance a businessman –

and I think there are some here with us building up their business, gaining and achieving something, is also reversing the entropy of the world. Any woman in this audience, cooking a good meal for her family, is also refusing to give up in order to build up something which is family life and love. So the courage is not abstract reality, philosophical thought, it is incarnated in each action I perform, it is a refusal to let go, to give up.

Through his body man emerges to humanity. I believe in this kind of incarnation, the courage to be passes through the body. I visited in Cairo once, near the pyramids of Ghiza, a ballet school. I saw kids from 6 to 12, boys and girls, learning ballet, six hours a day! From 8 to 2 in the afternoon they had exercises, trying to stand on the tips of their toes, performing movements which were difficult. After these 6 hours of ballet they had 2 or 3 hours of teaching, formal classes like all other kids. In these 2 or 3 hours of formal teaching they achieved higher standards than the others who had 6 hours of teaching a day. How come? Through their bodies they had learned concentration and attention. My conviction is that we can learn to master our minds through the body, in developing our consciousness. You can observe their tension, a concentration in the eyes of these trained kids which does not exist in the eyes of an untrained child. This is why I strongly believe in the power of human effort through the body. The courage to be passes through the body.

Sometimes we say that circumstances are against us, people are against us, therefore we are discouraged, tempted into despair. We don't realise that through obstacles man builds himself. The more obstacles you have before you, the more you are challenged to overcome them. You have two kinds of people: those who, confronted with an obstacle, say: "Oh, I'm finished, I can't." They just sit down and wait. The second kind of people are those who are challenged by the obstacle and say: "How do I overcome it?" They decide to surmount the obstacle and find a second level of being through it. The obstacle becomes a means of self-realisation, of evolving, of growing up.

(Ref K)

Whoever is inspired by the Spirit, can know things, can discover things, can understand things at a glance. He opens his eyes, he closes his eyes, he has seen, he has understood. This is the Spirit. The Spirit is capable of revealing in just one tiny sign what is hidden behind it. The power of the Spirit is to reveal the inner secrets of things. Others have to look and inquire and they still don't understand. But the inspired person catches the meaning of something at a glance, understands immediately, because he sees the reality from inside. You cannot penetrate the inner reality which you see with your eyes unless you are inspired by your inner eyes. From inside to inside. This is the only way of seeing.

This is what we also call faith. People around Jesus saw the miracles he performed, everyone heard the words he said. Some believed, some didn't. Why? How come? Take the Pharisees, the more miracles they saw the more they became hardened in their hearts, the more they opposed Jesus, the more they refused to believe. And this is exactly what made Jesus say:

"Do you not yet perceive or understand? Are your minds closed?

Have you eyes that do not see, ears that do not hear? Or do you not remember?"

(Mark 8, 17.18)

Understanding with the hearts! Faith is not a question of having great signs, great miracles, fantastic things before me. No, a tiny little sign is enough to believe. People expect an apparition of Our Lady or miracles by Jesus. They believe that should be then the rock on which to build their faith. True faith does not need that. We have so many signs around us. One thousand faces of the Spirit! One thousand signs of the Spirit. We just have to look and that is sufficient. We believe, we trust, we see, we feel, we have, we get the meaning and this is enough. This is faith.

I am not against exegetes. I am not against theologians. I am not against very clever people searching for the mystery of faith in long and complicated strides. But every theological search should be a search not only with the brain and with techniques, but with the heart and in prayer. Any theology should be written kneeling down. If not physically, at least internally, in a state of receptiveness, of prayer, of meditation, of contemplation. This is the way St. Thomas Aquinas wrote his *Summa Theologiae*. This is the way any theologian should write his books, books not inspired by the brain which few understands, but inspired by the heart which anybody can understand. I would say true theology should be at the level of everybody. This is why Jesus was understood by the simplest people. And true theologians speak a language which can be understood by anybody. The Fathers of the Church did not speak in big auditoriums with students of theology; they spoke to average people, peasants, workers, people in the street, not in big and beautiful churches. And this is why they were able to express things in an intelligible way.

Since I speak about faith and the deepening of faith, I should say something else. The expression of faith is endless. The search for meaning in faith is an endless process. We are never at the end of understanding faith. We are never at the end of understanding God. God is an abyss, an ocean, an infinity! Any theological system, any dogmatical build-up which pretends to have reached the wholeness of faith, the totality of faith, is a fake, and remains an illusion. This is why the Spirit pushes the Church to deepen and deepen our faith. But the danger for the Church is to think that at a certain point everything has been said, that there is a final point of theology. The Church once taught that the theology of St. Thomas Aquinas was the body, the complete body of Catholic theology. Fortunately, since Vatican II we have discovered that theology is an endless process and has one thousand faces, because the Spirit speaks in many tongues, in many ways, through many people, through many nations and cultures. We have the theology of Karl Rahner, we have the Theology of Liberation, we have the theology of Africa, we have the theology of the Middle-East, we have the theology of France today. There is not just one theology, there are many, each of them expressing one true aspect, or a certain view of the Christian mystery, of the Christian faith. They are different, but they should not be opposed, they are complementary views, aspects of the same and fathomless faith and truth.

(Ref G)

What makes faith seem so irrelevant nowadays? Because it does not answer the questions of our times. It should provide answers to the way we live today, in the same way as the Bible answered the questions of contemporary man. We must learn to read and interpret the signs of each period in history. This was one of the mainsprings of Vatican II, and today the Church must continue in this direction. Karl Marx tried to do this in his way. He built a whole system, Marxism, which unfortunately later became Communism. But Marxism is a 'Weltanschauung', a fascinating analysis of our society! It failed as an ideology but it has left us with a question mark. A great French theologian once said about Marxism..... "Communism is a Christian idea gone crazy." (Henri de Lubac, S.J.)

Basically it was a Christian idea! Socialism had already been applied by the early Christians. Sharing one's property and belongings, caring for the poor and trying to bring justice to them was intrinsic to the Gospels. Marx's idea did go awry, then let us invent something better on the same lines. It is a challenge, a call to the Church and to all Christians. See people rejoice and dance because of the fall of Communism and some welcome the rise of capitalism, but Francis Fukuyama (John Hopkins University, Washington) in his recent book "The End of History" claims that the triumph of the free market, of capitalism and liberalism, marks the end of history. What do we Christians say to this? What is our answer? The Islamists say:

"Communism has failed, capitalism is failing, we bring the answer.

We must all get back to God. Do not speak about human rights but about God's rights,

Do not speak about human law but about God's law, the 'sharia'.

We are longing to build a society based on Allah."

The emptiness, the void now existing in Europe, has driven many people towards Islam. Its teachings bring them a clear answer. Buddhism is also gaining ground in Europe and in America. Zen meditation, Yoga and Transcendental Meditation are fashionable nowadays. This re-emergence of religious movements is due to the lack of an ideology, the failure of spiritual answers it gives, and the nourishing of faith it provides. Buddhism is an answer for many but at the same time an escape for others. The whole of creation is just 'maya', it proclaims a world of illusion. Christian mysticism is not a flight from reality, it is built on the Incarnation of God. It is rooted in human reality and in daily life. It integrates and understands the importance of the concrete world, our world and our history, God's history yes, but he is at work in it, together with Man. It is our duty to get involved and to fight against Evil.

Coming as I do from Egypt I am often asked what my answer is to Islamism. I am not well informed of what is really going on in Europe, but I know for sure that the Islamists are aiming to conquer Europe. At all costs! They say that in 100 years the whole of Europe will be in the hands of Islam. They mean it, and while Christianity is fading away, Islam is taking its place. The European society of the future will be based on Sharia Law, a law which has not changed since the 9th century and is applied very strictly, even today.

Christ also gave us a law - to love one another. This is neither a system nor a code like the 10 Commandments. If you open the Old Testament and read Leviticus, how many laws? You have to wash your hands like this .. not in this way! But this law was made for very primitive people who needed to be instructed, and little by little the Mosaic Law evolved, and when we enter the New Testament we learn that there is only one law, one word: LOVE! You cannot make a law for the whole of mankind and for all times because, as I said before, history is changing and it will always change. Man also continues to evolve. You have to have an adaptable law, rooted in Man's nature and in the nature of the universe. The only law of the universe is love, within, behind and above all things. We Christians have to reinvent this love, not according to our old structures but to a modern way of life which will be new today but may be old tomorrow.

Is there a Christian form of statehood, is there a special form of Christian civilization? Is there a clear-cut, applicable Christian law, is there a form of Christian politics? No! Then we have no model? The Church says there is no such model, but

"we have an eternal source of inspiration: the Gospels, and we have an ideal: Christ."

We have guidelines, yes, some criteria, and principles, but no model for a state. The best analysis of the social, political, and economic situation of our times can be found in the papal encyclicals from the end of the 19th century until now (from Pope Leo XII to John Paul II). They do not give ready-made answers, but they are very clear on what is good and what is not good. Having studied these documents very carefully, and inspired by their vision, it is up to us all to play an active part in the shaping of a future society and its politics. With the help of prayer we must learn to distance ourselves from events in order to give full scope to our commitment. The Church cannot tell us which politician to vote for, she cannot tell us which economic system to choose. We ourselves have to reach a state of enlightenment in order to judge for our country and act with responsibility. Nothing is given once and for all, politics has to be reinvented every day, society too and your personal involvement. In the name of your faith you have to commit yourself to try to change this world for the better and build what Pope John Paul II calls a Civilization of Love.

Moses was looking after his sheep on Sinai when God suddenly spoke to him, sent him to the Pharaoh and asked him to liberate the Israelites in order that they could leave Egypt. Moses answered that he could not speak on their behalf, that he was not the right person for this job, and it would be much better to send his brother Aaron. But God insisted on Moses going. This is what happens with most of us! We are always looking for someone else to do the job, because we think they can do it better. Sending Moses to the

Pharaoh was a political action, and we have the mystical experience of the Burning Bush linked to it.

God reveals himself to Moses in a mystical way, and gives him a political mission.

Here we have the key! A conscious encounter with God means being sent somewhere to save humanity. During Moses' life there is this interplay between mystical experience and political mission, from up on the mountain to the people down on the plain.

This move from prayer to action, from mystical encounter to involvement in helping others, is what is asked from each of us. We receive the light, the impulse from God which is called inspiration, and we must transform it into a social commitment, political and civil engagement. The essential point is to know that God is with me just as he was with Moses when he sent him on his mission. It is not that I must throw myself into any project by myself, I cannot do much by myself. Today's challenges are so immense that they often make me feel helpless. But God tells me:

"Do not be afraid, ...now go and I will be with your mouth and teach you what you are to speak."

(Exodus 4, 12)

(Ref T)

THE BICYCLE

cf The parable of the weeds among the wheat

(Matthew 13, 24-30)

In these days Jesus sat with his friends on a coffee-house terrace and they discussed many things. And while they were talking, Jesus was watching a boy on the road below who was desperately trying to learn to ride a bicycle. He kept getting on, wobbling, toppling over and falling to the ground, and then, forcing himself to cling unto the saddle again, he would cling to the handlebars with all his might, swayed and rocked, only to fall off yet again. All his efforts were in vain. In the end he yelled angrily, "Why has the damn thing only got two wheels and not three, or better still four like a car.....!"

After a few more similar attempts, which always ended the same way, the boy resigned, put his bicycle aside and squatted at the roadside, while in front of him one of his friends drew the wildest loops on his bicycle, with great guts, leaning dangerously into the bends, defying the laws of gravity and logic. How was it that he didn't fall off? A complete riddle!

This is where someone needed a word of encouragement. Jesus got up, and leaving his friends, went down to help the beginner. He explained to him:

"The first rule: Boldness! Take the plunge! Cast aside all fears. Don't hesitate! Throw yourself forward and pedal hard! You'll only be able to keep your balance if you make headway smartly - in fact, you must fairly whiz along. Don't allow yourself even to think of falling and then you won't fall. As soon as you begin to doubt whether you'll make it - that is the end. Fear will quite definitely throw you out of the saddle. The second rule: Farsightedness! Always look straight ahead of you. Don't rivet your eyes on that wobbly front wheel. Keep them glued to the horizon and you'll find that you'll take off splendidly."

Then Jesus helped the boy to get back on his bicycle, gave him a good shove and shouted:

"Go on now! Chin up! Look straight ahead! Relax and trust! Pluck up your courage and make the dive!"

The boy shot forward like an arrow and disappeared behind the next bend. Jesus' friends had watched the scene from afar. When he got back and was among them again, he said:

"And now I will tell you the parable of the bicycle because it is a true master for Man. First it teaches him that an apparent fault or shortcoming is basically an advantage and therefore of great value. How much flexibility and speed would be lost if a bicycle had a third wheel! A tricycle is much more awkward to steer and therefore far less efficient."

At this point someone in the group interrupted him. "Can't one draw a parallel here to human beings who are lighter, quicker and more nimble on two feet than on all fours?" This example delighted Jesus and he said:

"Exactly! One could indeed ask why human beings, who are by no means light, should have to balance on two legs, when they would be so much steadier on all fours. And think of all those tears they shed as toddlers when they first learn how to walk! They would save themselves all those, too! But don't they continuously challenge the laws of equilibrium and gravity by walking upright? They certainly do! This is a call to overcome their purely human nature, indolent and protected as it is.

Yes, I wanted Man on two legs! So that he would be faced at an early age with the challenge of having to train hard and thereby learn to go beyond himself. Once that has been acquired it becomes second nature to him, a physical sign of his transcendence.

To glide along swiftly on two wheels and keep one's balance requires surpassing oneself. This challenge which certain laws of nature pose becomes even more pronounced in dance and ballet, when the body achieves weightlessness and, having become ethereal, scorns all the laws of physics and logic. Heroic mountaineering is another example of how a hostile object can captivate Man and inspire him to superhuman achievements. A child's performance on a bicycle is similar. By way of mastering this new skill, the child learns to outgrow himself."

"Such thoughts would never have occurred to me simply by looking at a bicycle!" a young girl said, shaking her head. And Jesus went on:

"That is by far not everything that I want to tell you about riding a bicycle. Looking forward with one's head held high, whether on foot or on a bicycle, is not only a physical phenomenon, it is also an attitude of mind. Only he who is far-sighted will get ahead. Only he who fixes his eyes on the horizon will achieve a lot. His own faltering glances downward will irritate him because they paralyse him from within. They take the wind out of his sails, make him wobble, make him fall. But he who has his eyes on the horizon will be drawn forward magnetically and will pick up speed. So throw yourselves forward towards your goal! You'll only make headway if you put your trust in the future - in what is yet to come. The further you dare to look, the more you will achieve. Be bold, my boy, and always be confident!

And now one last thing of particular importance for you, as it concerns faith. Joyfully swinging oneself on a bicycle is a blind act of faith, isn't it? It means laying a wager on the possible when all the odds are on the side of the impossible. In doing so you cross the zone of uncertainty and perform a miracle.

I have come to teach you faith, both in God and in yourselves. For there is only one faith in which everything meets and becomes united. Unfortunately, man has separated what belongs together, as if one faith contradicted the other.

Exactly the opposite is true. Man proves his confidence in God by trusting himself and by steadily developing his self-confidence, but always in the awareness that God is at work within him and with him. Hence his boldness, his serene mood, his composure and his peace of mind. I have implanted in every human being endless possibilities, but they can only unfold and develop according to his degree of self-confidence. Every time a human being risks something, this mystery is wonderfully revealed.

Do you remember my prophecy that one day you will be able to do greater things than I did? (John 14, 12) That will hold good. Yes, with my strength you will do greater things because this strength is always within you. If nothing is impossible to God ((Luke 1, 37), then nothing is impossible to man, as long as he hopes and believes."

(Ref L)

Chapter 8: Fear – or Love and Happiness?

We live in the age of insurances: social security, health insurance, pensions insurance, accident insurance, travel insurance, household insurance—and more. One is even insured with a life insurance in case of death—it seems like an insurance against death—because contemporary man has "angst." He asks society to protect him and to assure him with optimal security. In former times people were "insured" through the Church, who promised them eternity and sold them indulgences. Today insurance companies sell their policies because people no longer believe in eternity and the hereafter and want, at least for this life, certain guarantees. Man is forever possessed with the desire to protect and insure himself against everything.

We wanted to create a society of consumers, and now we have it! Through it, we sell ourselves on continually more refined nutritional products, and constantly more senseless beauty products, and even much more. A small window shopping excursion of Alexandria's Boulevard Saad Zaghloul .suffices for.us to understand the degree of slavery we have again achieved, in the meantime. The wide-open jaws of this monster-like "consumer society" is about to swallow us all. We have known all this for some time. Each one of us knows the game being played here, but everyone is joining in.

Yet another type of modern slavery is the tyranny of fashion today in the year of 1992 which dictates everything, even to the precise centimetre length, or width, of a very casual pair of jeans for a teenager! One has his prescribed role to play in order to be accepted and confirmed. And appropriate garments, or clothing, do speak their language - they are the advertisement. Man is a slave to the opinion of others. There are few people who have the courage to wear what pleases them and makes them feel comfortable, or who are indifferent to whatever "look" is presently dictated as "in".

Society has assigned us various roles, and each of us plays his role "religiously" according to its demands. It already begins, in the group formations of adolescence where a .twelve year old, not only dresses and behaves according to the opinion of his peer group, but also feels and thinks like the group. And as an adult, man does not become less of a slave to his surroundings. He also will dress and behave in keeping with those around him and he will feel and think like them. From early on he has been trained in cowardliness. He smoothes "the rough edges" to fit in and to be pleasing to public opinion; he becomes smooth and pliant. His personality is carefully kneaded into shape, even his vested thinking and his innate originality, so that he is able to adapt everywhere and easily swim with the flow. Afraid to be free -- to fear to be one's "self"!

(Ref M)

I think that fear nearly always comes from the devil. Fear does not come from God. This is why, when God speaks to someone in the Bible often the first thing he says is "Do not be afraid." When the angel Gabriel came to Mary he also said "Don't be afraid." Most important meetings in the Bible begin with "Don't be afraid...."

Fear blocks a person, blocks his energy, blocks his capacity for understanding, for hearing and for learning. One of the most important things for me is to help people overcome this, fear of others, fear of themselves, fear of life, fear of the future, fear of God. The old system raised people in fear in order to make them obedient, but this is not the right way. You cannot build spiritual life on fear. The signs of the Holy Spirit are love, joy, peace, patience, kindness, goodness, trustfulness, gentleness and self-control. Fear is the opposite.

There are good fears and bad fears, some fears are necessary. Fear is a normal process for defending oneself and resisting evil. Fear can produce a positive reaction. In the face of a physical aggressor you react immediately and you defend yourself. But fear should not become a kind of tautological, morbid attitude; this is something one has to overcome. When a problem is over, it's resolved, but some people remain stuck in it with a complex, fearful for years, caught up by fear. This is pathological. A mental, psychological or spiritual disease. Fear as a necessary reaction is in order but not as a state of being. If it lasts too long it becomes an obstacle to life.

This is why, in his Spiritual Exercises, St. Ignatius speaks of fear in the first week of the exercises which is the week of purification of the soul. A certain fear of evil, of the devil, even of God in the sense of fire and punishment, a certain sense of sin - they can all be positive in the first step. Afterwards, when you enter into real spiritual life, fear fades away. The first steps on a religious path may require fear, but we should not act out of fear, but out of love. The negative aspect is not the right behaviour, even with animals when they are being trained. Trainers have discovered that in order to get better results you have to give them sugar and kindness instead of beating them. They improve through positive input, encouragement and incentives rather than punishment. The same results were achieved with children. Positive incentives are far better than the fear of punishment. The same applies to growth in spirituality.

(Ref N)

Love lies in the very nature of man, of all human beings. You have two tendencies in man: the self-centred tendency, which we call egocentrism, and the other tendency, which we call love, or the sexual impulse. And these two tendencies represent two stages in human life. The first stage is the stage of childhood. The child is self-centred, egocentric, which is normal. But God has placed within us the other tendency, which we call the sexual instinct that normally appears in adolescence. This helps the human being to go beyond himself, to start loving, to open himself towards a broader reality.

So through this movement we reproduce exactly the same movement which is within God, who realizes himself in extasis. When we live love, we come to know God. Knowing God is not respecting him, and thinking of him the way we did by trying to find out what the concept of God might be. No, knowing God is experiencing LOVE which reveals to us, by this very experience, the nature of God. God is an experience before being a concept. We always think of God as a philosophical concept - that is how to understand God in an abstract way. That is alright, you can do this. But this God fades away very soon, because he only exists in our brains. God has to become a living experience! And this is why St. John, in his first epistle, says very clearly:

"God is love, and anyone who lives in love lives in God, and God lives in him:"

(I John 4,16)

And he knows God. So if we love, it is God who loves in us. When we love, it is the Spirit who expresses himself through us, in us. God is personally continuing his own experience through every loving heart. And he enjoys it! The joy of God is when his Spirit crosses our human heart to develop this movement of love.

So to glorify God is not to take incense and say to Him: "You are great, you are the Almighty"; or to bow down and kiss the earth and say: "I adore you." You can do that, it's not forbidden - but the true cult, the true form of worship is to let him express himself through our hearts, through our human lives.

And this is why at the core of Christendom, you have one commandment, only one: LOVE. Loving is not something which is very clearly defined, but something spontaneous and difficult to fulfil. I spoke about the sexual instinct as a way of moving out of oneself, of giving oneself. But in the sexual instinct you also have the slight tendency to bring the other person to yourself as a kind of annexation. This is why the sexual instinct, which is a calling to love, can also be a kind of egoistic movement, a selfish movement to consume the other as you consume an apple. This is why the great Austrian Poet Rainer Maria Rilke said:

"It takes a long time learning to love"

Sometimes we think it's simple, it means just letting yourself go. But to love can be a never-ending effort. We have to learn it. In this experience, religion and life come together, they meet. And we cannot separate a religion of worship from a life of love. Nor can we understand human love and creation without understanding the real and true life of God. Through life and love you can understand God, and through God you can understand life and love.

(Ref D)

In the same way I have a mission, I have a job to do: I have my very own vocation in this society. I can't say: "If I don't do it, somebody else will." No, this somebody else does not exist. I have to do my duty, carry out my mission, and this gives to my life its density, its seriousness. My life is a serious matter, my life is important and my being is important and serious. I should not behave like the servant in the Gospel who took his talents and buried them in the ground. So many things are waiting to be developed within me, so many hidden talents, so many possibilities given to me which I am responsible for, not only for my sake but for humanity. One day I will be asked about these matters, and if I miss my vocation I miss what God expected me to do.

I would like to point out that you are more than you appear to be. Within your person there is the whole of humanity longing to "become". In each human being there is a kind of nostalgia for something greater that what he is, which he will never be able to realize in the frame of his own individual life, because his life is too short and his being seems too small. I have within myself the dream and the longing of being everything, of being all of you. I cannot achieve it, but you should achieve it! And then, when I speak of escaping from my Ego in order to open myself to you, I cross the fixed boundaries of my Self to open myself to a reality far greater which is called love. Love is losing oneself in order to find the whole of humanity. This is why love is a self-denial and self-accomplishment, self-denying because I lose my small Ego, I lose it, I cross the boundary of my Ego. I forget about myself and I find everything and everybody! The secret of love is the secret of a Whole Self, a Total Being! And this is why the secret of life is love. The secret of life is losing the Self in order to find the Whole. This is why Jesus said: "Love one another, this is my Commandment". This is the key to your life and this is the key to the Kingdom.

(Ref K)

In order to demonstrate the contrast between aesthetics and true religious art and true beauty, whether mystical or spiritual, I would like to make a comparison between Greek art and Byzantine art. In Greek art you have formal beauty - Apollo, Aphrodite - and all the beautiful statues we know. Fascinating! But in a certain sense, Greek art draws you out of the object's beauty; you contemplate the statue as formal beauty alone, whereas in Byzantine art, the beauty points to the heart and to the beyond. Through it you penetrate something which is of a different order, a different category. This piece of art is not an end in itself, it points to something else.

As a beginning we can try to understand how beauty is related to love. The world around us -the forest, the meadows with flowers, the sky, the birds, human beings, all these creatures and their whole spectrum, the texture of them, is love. God's love has taken shape in objects we see around us, and it is because they are created of love that they are beautiful. The beauty of a creature is the shining light of an inner love by which they have been shaped and formed and made. This relationship between beauty and love is very important in our reflection because love has generated beauty, and beauty can generate love in us. The contemplation of beauty has a magical effect on a person because it brings forth from his or her soul a feeling which we call love, there is no other word to express this feeling. Therefore there is a kind of dialectic between God's love shaping things and creatures, and expressing himself in them; and this recognised beauty leads man back to God.

Beauty is genuine food for the soul, it nourishes your body. Food which is not tasty, which is unpalatable, cannot be digested. Man needs beauty just as he needs food. We drink in as much beauty as we eat food. A world deprived of beauty is an inhuman world. Beauty creates mystical communion, with the reality before you. You feel yourself in union, one with the object which attracts you. This unity with reality has two effects. It brings a reality at a higher level of being because this reality takes a "surplus" (and you will taste it!) out of the natural realm, to a personal, spiritual, and human level. Therefore, contemplating beauty is a way of raising the natural world to the human and spiritual level.

In exactly the same way as food becomes yourself, becomes your life, becomes your thought, and love and inspiration, in the same way beauty enters into your self and becomes a part of yourself, lending growth to your inner being. The comparison between food and beauty works exactly, food makes you more human and allows you to listen to me now and to think and to feel. Beauty at another level generates more humanity in man. In participating in this plan, you fulfil your vocation and your mission in the world which is to bring forth creation to a higher level. As St. Paul says in his epistle to the Romans:

"The whole creation is eagerly waiting for God to reveal his sons."

(Rm. 8, 19)

This means that all creation and creatures are looking forward to human beings to raise them up from the natural and lower level to the human level, in order to accomplish themselves through us, and in accomplishing their potential they realise their goal.

(Ref R)

THE ILLEGAL IMMIGRANT

cf. Jesus' Arrest

(John 18,1-11)

In these days Jesus was arrested.

With incredible difficulty he had managed to make his way to Paris a few months previously, only to find himself without a roof over his head, without money or papers. An illegal immigrant and of course jobless. His Palestinian nationality and his leathery complexion made him particularly vulnerable he felt, far more so than the fact that he had no fixed address, as there were more than enough homeless in Paris. He was certain to be at the mercy of the first police raid that found him out. Added to which it was winter in Europe.

Constantly in fear of being caught, and exhausted from hunger and cold, it was above all the terrible loneliness in this capital city which almost suffocated him. He soon realised that the few words of French he had managed to pick up in his own country were of no use to him at all.

He understood no-one here and no-one understood him. He had nowhere to lay his head. (Luke 9, 58b) At night he sought shelter in the underground stations and slept on the benches there.

One night another poor wretch slept on the bench next to his and in the morning they were able to chat in Arabic, as the man was an Egyptian. He, too, was an illegal immigrant.

"My name is Nabil. Come back home with me, even if it is only an eighteen-foot-square

attic room on the fifth floor of an old house on the outskirts of Paris."

"Do you live alone?"

"There are four of us and unfortunately there is only one bed and a thick rug on the floor beside it. We sleep in relays depending on whether or not any of us gets a job. Occasionally I come back here like last night and sleep on a bench."

"Stop! How can you possibly manage a fifth person?!"

"We need each other. To talk. That is important. You'll be our fifth and you're welcome!"

Jesus climbed up the steep stairs to the fifth floor with Nabil. The little room was stuffy but warm and littered with four people's belongings. Plates, glasses and saucepans were piled up on the window sill. There was one chair and a small cupboard. And there was a petroleum stove for the most important thing of all - hot, sweet tea ...! The other attic rooms were all rented out to foreigners and full to overflowing. Altogether there were perhaps thirty Africans, Latin Americans and Asians up there.

Nabil said: "The crazy thing about this house is its incredible emptiness. It's a ghost house. Will that worry you? All the floors, with the exception of the ground floor, are empty and the flats securely locked. They say they belong to middle-class Parisians who hold on to them as second flats but you never see them here as they live in the better districts where life is pleasanter."

The group introduced Jesus to a man who traded in exotic products so that he could earn just enough to cover the bare essentials needed to survive. Bags of spices, nuts, silk flowers, cheap scents and very mediocre embroidery. Jesus was to try and sell this merchandise with a little profit for himself. Every day he packed his bag and ran to the underground because he knew his way round there. Having spread out his goods on a piece of cloth, he offered them for sale - and waited. Very often he waited in vain all day. Leaning against a wall, he stood there and waited. People rushed past him, indifferent, occasionally glancing absent-mindedly at the things he had to sell. Not so much because they were interested, but out of curiosity or amusement. And every time Jesus held his breath - wondering anxiously: will they buy something? Or will they leave it lying there? But the conversation was always the same: "How much?" "So many francs." "No thanks."

The passer-by was soon lost in the crowd and no doubt had not the slightest idea that had he purchased just one small item, Jesus could have bought the baguette he had been thinking of for hours.

The hours passed monotonously - and nothing happened! Nothing! But one evening, as Jesus squatted next to the products which interested no-one, and was about to begin to put them away, a stout, elderly gentleman stopped in front of him. The look in this foreigner's dark eyes seemed to him to reflect an intense weariness of life and great physical exhaustion. And so he bent down quickly and picked up an assortment of items from the cloth for the price of two hundred francs. While he was paying the eyes of the two men met and held each other's gaze for a few seconds. They did not speak. Jesus had great difficulty in holding back his tears.

After he had left his usual spot, lugging the large bag of unsold goods on his shoulders, he walked past an African in whose eyes he recognised that very same urgent need which he had felt up to a moment ago. So he went over to his brother immigrant and bought something from him for a hundred francs. The man's face was immediately transformed! His white teeth flashed and a huge smile lit up his shining brown face. Like Jesus, this young man had spent the entire day here and reaped nothing but indifference. Back in his shelter his wife and small child were waiting for the few francs that would buy them a frugal meal.

Those were Jesus' first weeks in Paris. Later on one of his comrades managed to find him a job as a kitchen boy. At long last guaranteed meals! That alone made up for everything. And a regular income, even if it was far below the legal minimum - but then he was an illegal immigrant and saw it as a big step forward. Not that it was easy to manage now either. He had to leave the house before sunrise and travel two hours to his work-place and hardly ever got back much before midnight. When he finally did get to the attic room, the bed and the rug beside it had long since been occupied. Two of his friends worked night-shifts. A narrow space between the cupboard and the wall was all that was left for him.

One evening, as he stood waiting for his bus, shaken by a cold, a police car drew up next to him abruptly. No hope of escape. "Your papers!" a voice bellowed out of the car window. Jesus still did not have any papers. Who should have wanted to give him any? He was arrested and rushed off to prison. There he found himself in the company of about fifty fellow sufferers from the so-called Third World who were being forced to lead a non-existence here. Now Jesus was among them. We all go to the dogs here, he thought ...

In these days Jesus jotted down the following thoughts and signed them. One day they will be found on a crumpled piece of paper in his pocket.

"After the hell of loneliness and unemployment, after the nightmare of the underground stations and restaurant kitchen, now a new hell - prison. I admit, however, that I prefer these existential experiences to the perfection of heaven with all my "angel comforts". Here I can share the situation of these suffering people - being an illegal immigrant as they are.

Could one ever believe in a God of Love, living in his far away heavenly realm, so far above such abject despair? And yet fully aware of these miserable creatures and their feelings? Will they not perish from rejection, vermin and the betrayal of their lives? There is no way back to their homelands either. I have listened to each of their stories.

Consistency is the principle and the demand. But how difficult it is to be consistent! What should I have done? How could I have done better or made myself clearer? How otherwise could I have really experienced what millions of people have to endure in their lives today, if I hadn't become Man myself again and suffered all in their midst as they do with body and soul? If, with compassion, I hadn't become one of them right here in prison, being one of these surely most forsaken people on earth at the moment, because literally abandoned and forgotten by the entire world?

So it is good to be here. There is nothing to regret, ever! I say YES YES again - and forever. And I sign:

Jesus – Immanuel"

(Ref L)

Chapter 9: Love and Immortality

An Interview between Father Henri Boulad, S.J. and Mag. Johannes Kaup at the ORF Radio Studio, Vienna 16 July 2007

KAUP: Father Boulad, for centuries, perhaps even for thousands of years, people have been longing to be immortal, to overcome death. What is immortality and how would you define it? Is it about the survival of the soul?

BOULAD: There are different ways of conceiving immortality - as the survival of the soul, which is a Greek concept, or a sort of survival of life which is a Pharaonic view, or a kind of survival of body and soul as in the early period of the Old Testament - what they called the Sheol. It's not exactly hell in the modern sense; it's the underworld, called Hades in Greek, and Infernon in Latin. It was a kind of underground area where the dead survived, half alive and half dead. Finally, in the last period of the Old Testament, probably under the influence of Greek thought, they discovered what we call the resurrection of the body which is, finally, a Christian concept. We Christians do not believe in the immortality of the soul alone; we believe in the resurrection of the body also, given that the human being is not a soul; he or she is body and soul in its complexity. The Christian vision of eternal life is seen through the phenomenon of the resurrection of the body, whatever this may imply.

In his theological writings, Karl Rahner has said that you cannot imagine human happiness without it being shared with the body. The body is part of our nature; we are not angels, so the concept of immortality of the soul is not a Christian concept. The association of the body in this eternal life is a dogma; it's part of the Creed, the last part of the Creed. But how should we conceive the body associated with the soul, or rather with the spirit? This is a controversial question, an open question.

KAUP: It's an open question in answer to which modern science adds new thoughts about death. Are there really new insights from modern natural sciences in conceiving the body and the soul, compared to former centuries?

BOULAD: Yes, modern science has discovered new kinds of matter which we call anti-matter or an energy which is partly matter. This opens new horizons to imagining other kinds of matter which are also called matter, because they are electrons spinning around a positive nucleus. But antimatter is the opposite. Nobody knows what kind of matter it is. It opens up a completely new world, but I think that science is unable to go beyond this very materialistic vision which should be superseded by a philosophical, metaphysical vision, or even a religious and mystical vision which goes far beyond that.

KAUP: Before we go any further I would like to ask why people dream of being immortal when everyone knows that death is the only thing we are certain of.

BOULAD: Of course, we are absolutely sure that we will die; people have known this since the beginning of life on earth around three million years ago. There is a feeling, no; it's more than a feeling, a conviction that the human being is called to an after-life. We have some proof of that; one proof is the burial of the dead. The dead were buried in a kind of urn which symbolises a woman's womb, the matrix, in a foetus-like position, contracted within itself, looking towards the Orient, towards the sunrise. This shows that people understood death as a rebirth of the human being, expecting another life in death, with this life being a kind of introduction to something else. Another indication is that they are looking towards the sunrise, the Orient, the East, meaning that they are expecting a new sun, a new life on the horizon. But why? It's probably in the nature of human beings to believe in immortality because it is our vocation. This cannot exist by mere chance.

I can put it another way. The compass pointer indicates the direction north but no-one has ever seen the north; it's a conclusion we reach that somewhere there is a north because the compass pointer is turning towards it. In the human soul there is a desire for immortality which shows that this desire cannot be born in our soul except through a reality which attracts it. There is a saying in medieval philosophy - "Non potest desiderium humane esse inanis." Human desire cannot be vain. Since there is a desire, there is, somewhere, a reality through which this desire will be fulfilled. For me it's part of human nature to strive or to dream or to achieve immortality.

KAUP: But as we are modern and analytical thinkers, especially when you think of psychoanalysis, then Sigmund Freud would probably say: "Maybe there is a desire but it could be wishful thinking." It could be some kind of ideal that is exalted as a kind of superego because we are so scared that we somehow invent immortality in order to soothe ourselves, so that we can live with the horrible reality of our coming death. What do you think of the possibility that it is just wishful thinking?

BOULAD: I would say that there is no definite proof of immortality. We may try, but we will never find any proof. Immortality is an act of faith, but faith based on a kind of reasonable thinking. I would call it rational thinking. It's reasonable thinking. We have to distinguish between rational thinking and reasonable thinking. I would add that the Western way of thinking is severely handicapped because it uses only the left side of the brain. In the West, you are analytical people; you are shaped by your analytical minds, by reason or science. If the brain has a right side which is intuition, feeling, thinking which is not linked to the brain, then I would call it non-logical thinking. What is illogical for you may be logical. It means something which is beyond the mind, and people are discovering this aspect more and more nowadays. It makes sense to them. Post-modernity has moved away from modernity. Modernity is based on reason, on facts, on science. Post-modernity is a kind of return to a holistic approach, and to the truth which we call wisdom. I think that if we use our whole being, and our whole brain, we will find that this approach is totally reasonable. I would say that it is this hypothesis that renders sense to human life, and "makes sense", although it has not been proven. But a hypothesis can be proven by the fact that something is explained, just as in mathematics. In mathematics you say."Let's suppose that a = b". It's a supposition, a hypothesis at the beginning. But, if you can prove that a = b at the end of your equation, it means that a really does equal b. It is no longer a hypothesis, because it has been possible to make sense of the puzzle which you are trying to solve.

From my point of view, the after-life, immortality, is something which makes sense and gives sense to human life, to human desire, connected to this thought from the Middle Ages - "Non potest desiderium humane esse inanis." Another point is that no human life achieves itself in the frame of the eighty or ninety years that we live on earth. It's a kind of severing, a movement searching for an accomplishment, and this accomplishment is contradicted by what we call death. Death is an absurdity, since it is a kind of interruption of some development. We have to postulate immortality. I like the word postulate — it means affirming something which has not been proven, but we have to postulate it in order to explain a phenomenon. So we have to postulate an after-life, a continuation until this life is really fulfilled. Before scientists discovered Pluto, the last planet of our solar system, they found some strange phenomena and they postulated that the planet must exist in a certain place, until they found it. So a postulation was reasonable. We have been able, scientifically, to identify this planet, to see it and to study it.

KAUP: How would you react, for example, to a person who says that if you postulate something it is still a kind of wishful thinking, and you cannot insist on the fact that life is just confined in this small framework. It is not whole and it is not fulfilled. It is just a series of trial and error, fragments. There is no sense behind it except that you live it, and try to live a good life. What do you think of this?

BOULAD: I think that Teilhard de Chardin brings a very convincing argument. He says that if the human being did not believe that his life was worth living, he would die immediately. There is an instinct, unconscious, unknown, within us which makes us eat and sleep, breathe and survive. Unconsciously, within our being, we have a strong striving towards life which is proof that this life leads somewhere. This argument about the individual is also an argument about the whole of mankind. Mankind's striving towards progress, towards a kind of outgrowing of oneself means that somewhere there is a pole which pulls humanity forward on tracks, beyond the stage we are now in. Whether at the level of the individual, of history or humanity, you have this strong drive towards the realisation of the self. Since death means a cutting off of this movement, we can presume or postulate an after-life which is a continuation of this life.

KAUP: Let's turn to the Bible, to Jesus Christ. What does he say about immortality?

BOULAD: We can find many texts about immortality in the New Testament, about the resurrection and about life after death. You have the parables of Lazarus and of the rich young man which clearly indicate that there is an after-life. You can call it heaven and hell; there is certainly something beyond this life. When he was crucified, Jesus also spoke to the thief on his left side about the resurrection, saying: "Today you will be with me in paradise." When Lazarus rose from the dead, he said "Whoever believes in me, he will live, even if he is dead. I am the resurrection and the life." In the gospels there are many texts showing that Jesus speaks of a paradise, an after-life or resurrection. There are also many texts in St Paul's writings which speak about our resurrection. It's clear that Christianity or the gospel indicate that there is something beyond.

KAUP: What is meant by paradise? What is meant by resurrection, the way towards paradise? What can we say by contrast to what the myths are saying?

BOULAD: I have a vision about this reality which we call paradise, heaven, immortality or resurrection. I'll put it like this: there is only one man who started with Adam and who will be completed at the end of history. This man developed his potential through what we call humanity. Each of us is a concrete expression of one of the billion possibilities contained in this first seed called Adam. Adam is the seed of mankind, and this seed, in order to become explicit, has to develop in what we know as generations and generations of human beings. You and I are examples of the concrete realisation of this potential of humanity contained in Adam. That includes all the human beings on earth today, and all the human beings who existed in the past, and who are living in us, in us - the dead are not living in a different world! Dying means continuing one's life within the living people on earth, and pushing this movement forward, a movement which will attain its fulfilment at the end of history. At that moment the whole number of human beings will be united in one reality which Teilhard de Chardin called the Omega point. This Omega point is the realisation of Adam, the first Adam who carried humanity in him in an implicit way, unconsciously. You and I were in Adam, unconsciously, implicitly. We have been given the chance of living our lives.

This life is the movement from the implicit to the explicit, from the unconscious to the conscious, from the impersonal to the personal. The movement of evolution is the unfolding of a potential human being to a real human being. This human being is the totality of mankind, collected in one point which is the second Adam. The second Adam is the first Adam totally personalised.

This is the fullness of love. For me, immortality is related to love when the total sum of human beings will be united in such a way, deeply and existentially. We will have a body, an idea which you will find mentioned in St Paul's epistles, the body of humanity, the new Adam, finally realised, in that sense. I always speak of the sixth day of creation when God is said to have created Man. We are living in the sixth day. In that sense, the seventh day has not arrived yet. We are still in the sixth day. Man is being woven on the loom now, created; we are realising human-kind which is the purpose of creation or, scientifically spoken, of evolution.

For me, the former generations, people who have died, survive in me, and you, and in humanity present on earth. They are pushing forward, and, for generation after generation, this humanity is being built on one unity, one humanity. When this humanity has achieved its fulfilment, this means resurrection, which is the turnover of the inside to the outside, from the implicit to the explicit, of all past history and of mankind from all the generations who have ever lived will be really present and live within us. It will be a major crisis which will be the birth of mankind, the birth of humanity. What we call the end of mankind is the birth of mankind, called resurrection. There will be no individual resurrection. The resurrection will be a cosmic event, a total event, where all humanity will be gathered in one body, and will emerge in this total fulfilment of eternal life. Eternal life is not an individual process or an individual reality but a collective experience. There is only one history and one humanity, and we are all part of it, and if life is supposed to overcome death, it's through this collectivity of a love stronger than death as it is said in the Canticle of Canticles. Love is stronger than death. I believe that, in this process of building up generation after generation, the body of humanity is what is pointing to this further state, the final state in which death will be engulfed in life, engulfed in love, and, finally, the triumph of love which will overcome. Love is the secret of life, the depth of life, because love is the search for unity.

KAUP: You said that we are all part of one humanity, one body and it is about resurrecting this second Adam. But what about our individuality, our individual lives? Do they matter? This is what mankind desires! Overcoming death must not mean becoming a drop in the ocean. Man still wants to live, to feel, to realize his potential, and he still wants to be recognised.

BOULAD: Of course! I am happy about this question because the Asian way of thinking, whether in Hinduism or in Buddhism, is that we are just a drop in the ocean, and we appeared in order to disappear, and to melt in this huge soup (sorry about the expression) which will swallow up all our individualities in order to become Brahman or Atman or Nirvana, thus discarding what is most personal in each person. This is, of course, not the Christian way which is utterly personal. And this personal aspect is essential for thinking about this body, about this immortality. Each of us will be himself to the utmost. We will not find this immortality in going backwards; it is in going forward, as Teilhard de Chardin puts it, that the union personalises.

And this is the difference between union and unity, because unity can be ambiguous. Unity can mean what you have just said, a kind of melting pot or merely drowning in this ocean, and losing what makes us personal: our identity. But there is a super-identity to be found in this union which will combine the totality of mankind in me. I will inherit all the potential and possibilities of people in all generations which will become me, myself, and I will give them my little self in order to complete them. Actually, I am Adam, you are Adam. Adam is in me as a dream, as a longing to become. But I will remain myself. When I am Adam it means I will be myself when I have become the totality of mankind. My vocation is not just to be Henri, it is to be Henri, and to be Christ.

What is meant by Christ? The mystical Christ is the

perfect man accomplished. You also find it in Islamic Sufism. They call it the perfect man. You find it in the Greek tradition; they called it poinandros. Poinandros is the perfect man. St. Paul's perfect man, who is the mystical Christ, has also been perceived by other religions, including in Hinduism where Atman is the perfect man, the perfect personality. But, comparing that with Christianity, the real difference is that this collective personality in Christ will finally fulfill our longing for being ourselves. Of course, it's difficult to imagine being myself to the utmost, and being united with all others in order not to be swallowed up. As Teilhard de Chardin puts it - "Love and union super-personalise." It's a super-personalisation.

The differences between Christianity and the Eastern religions or philosophies concern this point because Christianity says that we emerge in an impersonal world in order to personalise it. And since evolution is a process, a forward-looking process, superseding itself, maturing, it cannot go backwards, it must go forward, and forward means spiritualisation, personalisation, humanisation. Teilhard de Chardin would say an "amorisation". For me, this vision is much more significant, rational or more reasonable than to say that this world has no meaning; everything ends up in nothingness; we are all condemned to death. If this is the case, then my life is meaningless, because if my life ends in death, what is the meaning of it? If I am not a part of this cosmic evolution as an essential element, then why, why live? What was the point of my existence if only to end up in a dark hole called the tomb.

In my opinion, the tomb is just the beginning. I think that those people whom we call primitive, understood death as putting a seed in the ground. These people were in close contact with nature. And nature calls us; it shouts at us. Life and death are the same thing. It's a kind of transformation, of metamorphosis, of evolution. When you put a seed in the ground and it decays and dies, it means that it is the beginning of a tree, of a new life. But we city dwellers who have lost our natural roots, may not perceive life except artificially. We have lost the sense for life after death, and life through death, and a new morning after the night, just as spring comes after the winter. We have lost the meaning of this cosmic cycle, embedded as we are in a technical and electronic world. We don't realise the mystery of the cosmos which is a continuous transformation. There is nothing which indicates total death. The people of China, with their concept of Tao, the concept of life and death, black and white have the same idea. There is no such thing as an ending in death. Life is transformed.

KAUP: What role does love play in this process? How is love linked to immortality in a Christian sense?

BOULAD: In my opinion, in the deepest sense, it indicates two or three pathways. Firstly, if immortality is the gathering of all mankind in one, then this force, this energy, which pushes each individual to outgrow himself or herself, to supersede himself or herself, is called love. Sexuality, which is the desire of the other, is the beginning of what we call love. It's the embeddedness of love in the body; it's part of the hormonal system. It means that we cannot achieve ourselves except through another person. This sexual drive in us points to a deep longing for the completion of each other. We are not yet perfect human beings, we are promises, projections of man accomplished. Love is this deep drive in us which compels us to outgrow ourselves in order to achieve ourselves in another person. You are a part of me, and I am a part of you. As long as we fail to unite, we will not accomplish our whole selves. What is expressed in human love is the deepest meaning of life. Life is a longing for completion, for accomplishment. Love plays **the** essential role of uniting all the human molecules with each other in order to realise, to achieve this final body. I would call love a cosmic force which is the means of achieving this completion of the body of mankind.

KAUP: What kind of love are you talking about? Do you mean human love?

BOULAD: Human love, of course, yes, but human love aiming for another love which is called Agape. There is Eros, Agape and Filia. The three are one, finally, because Agape means losing oneself for the other, forgetting oneself for the sake of the other. This already exists in Eros, but Eros has to supersede itself in order to reach its goal which is Agape, or Filia which is a kind of social attraction to each other experienced deeply in human love. And then, as Teilhard de Chardin wrote and explained it, love is a basic energy of the cosmos. It manifests itself in the atom; this attraction between protons and electrons is already love. This tropism and tactism in animal life is already love; this drive pushes all the elements of the cosmos to each other in order to achieve unity. The last word in evolution is unity. The words unity and universe have the same stem, from uni - one. The oneness of the world is inscribed in its origin, and it is inscribed in its end, in its goal, in its final goal — UNIVERSE. And since we are speaking about this after-life, I would add that the idea of the university is not honest to itself if it does not provide a unified vision of the cosmos for its students. If the university is not an answer to the universe, which means a world seeking unity, it fails its vocation which is often the case nowadays. The university has always been a place where people became specialised, but this is just a part of it. The university should offer a global vision of life, of existence, otherwise it betrays its goal.

KAUP: You have just spoken about the link between human love and divine love, but what is the link between love and existence, and love and creation. How are they connected?

BOULAD: We are the product of an act of divine love. God dreamt of me. He dreamt of you, he loved me before I existed, that is why I exist. His love has been embodied in what I am since time immemorial. I am an act of love made flesh. Furthermore, I am related to this act of love at every moment of my existence. I survive, I subsist because God creates and loves me at each moment anew. Divine love is not something abstract for me, it is not that he loves me from afar with a telescope or by e-mail contact. No, my life, my whole existence, is an act of subsisting divine love. I have developed this idea in many of my writings and books. I believe that just as the earth is the solid ground of my physical being, love is the spiritual realm of my total being. I experience God's love is as solid as a rock. The word rock is just a physical expression, a concrete expression of what God's love is.

The relationship between love and existence is an existential relationship. My existence has no reality, has no justification except through the total existence of this Infinite Being which we call God. It is only he who really exists, totally and really, God! My existence is borrowed through his existence. He gave me part of what he is. In other words, I HAVE existence. He IS existence. The only difference is between having and being. I have existence. I received it from the one who is himself existence. He is the Being; I have being. He is life; I have life. As long as human beings fail to understand this phenomenon, they can insist on being atheists, or their agnosticism. These are just words. Agnosticism and atheism are unwise and empty as far as I am concerned, I'm afraid to say. Man has to find a meaning to his being. What is the meaning of your existence? You exist, but how and why? The only answer is to relate your being to an absolute reality which is the being. The eternal absolutely necessary being. This is the difference in philosophy between contingency and necessity. I am contingent to reality. This contingency cannot justify itself except through something which is absolutely necessary.

I would like to add something about the relationship between love and immortality. Love can be a proof for me, not a scientific proof, but an existential proof of immortality. If you love someone, from the bottom of your heart, you cannot imagine that one day this girl or this woman with her flesh and blood, her eyes, her smile and personality could simply disappear, return to nothingness. You cannot even begin to imagine that.

I had an experience of this kind when I was fourteen years old. I was the leader in a scout organisation and I was looking after 30 ten-year-olds. One of them died in an accident in the sea near Alexandria. He died tragically, and, for the first time in my life, I saw a corpse, a dead body, so fresh, as though alive, lying on his bed, and his mother beside him, speaking to him as though he were still alive. She couldn't believe or conceive that this boy of hers was dead. She simply couldn't. For her, this little boy was not dead, he was alive in some way, she could not imagine or explain it, but kept talking to him. She did not cry because she knew, deep in her heart, that this little boy was alive somewhere and somehow. I remember it vividly although it was sixty years ago; I still have this picture before my eyes.

For me, loving somebody is telling him: "You cannot die." Loving somebody is telling him: "You cannot die. You will never die." This is the existential proof each of us has to prove it for himself, because no-one can transmit it to another person. Try to imagine your son, your daughter, your wife, your husband dying. Can you imagine that this person has disappeared forever, as though he/she has returned to nothingness, to zero? I cannot even imagine it for myself. I cannot imagine that Henri Boulad will cease to exist. No, I cannot. I know that I will live forever. This is what I call an existential proof. Modern people are caught up in the snares of what we call reason or science. I call it snares because it is a very dangerous way of thinking, putting aside what we call existence or existential thinking. If we do not return to existential thinking in a holistic way, we are going astray, we are losing the true way of thinking.

KAUP: I have a final question. What does this mean for our lives, living in the presence of death, but with the desire and hope of being immortal? How does this affect our personal lives, how should we live if we cannot believe that we are immortal? And how to live this unique individual part? No-one can live for me. I cannot be replaced like a battery.

BOULAD: I would like to say two things. Firstly, my capacity for love is immensely important because it is a share of mankind which is dependent on me in order to accomplish it. To love is my vocation. It's my job! Living one's life is doing one's job, it is exactly like working in a factory. If each worker does his job well, you will have a fine car at the end of the production line. Doing my job as a human being is accomplishing ALL of my vocation, all my potential which is deep inside me. In order to develop myself to the utmost, to live my life as deeply as possible, and to the full, means that I have that obligation. This is my duty. This is what I get paid for. My life is my salary which has to be accomplished. This is one factor.

The other factor is my conviction that I will never die. This gives me deep, deep peace of mind and soul, of body and spirit. I am fully confident that I will never, never, never disappear. And whatever happens, I am always on the up and up, as I said in my book "All is Grace" which had been translated into 7 languages. All is grace, no matter what happens! I am always gaining. I live in a deep inner peace, with a deep inner optimism, a deep inner hope because I believe that nothing can affect me. These two points — firstly involving myself deeply in what I am doing, and trying to do my best, and living my life to the utmost. Secondly, deep peace and hope as well as enjoyment because life has meaning; life makes sense. Additionally, a third point - to love as much as I can because love is the basis of existence. The more I love the more I build up this body. The more I live and love, the more I participate in building a body which gives a goal to my life. It's fantastic!

Having a goal (I would call it a great design.) makes your life meaningful. It gives you impetus. It gives you dynamism. It gives you energy. It lends you genius because you know that you are doing something. You can achieve something great. But immortality is not merely gaining one's personal and individual life, immortality is something much bigger, huge; it involves the whole of humanity, and the whole of the cosmos. It is beyond our imagination. This is why St. Paul says in his first epistle to the Corinthians: "What the eye has not seen, and the ear has not heard, and the heart has not imagined, this is what God has prepared for those who love him." We cannot put it in words or figures. It's beyond all of that, but this beyond is more real to me than the table I am leaning on. This beyond is a reality. This is what I call faith, but faith not only in the religious sense but in the existential sense. Faith is believing in the sense of life, in a meaning for human life, in human evolution and divine mystery, in an ultimate mankind and cosmos. Existence has a meaning.

KAUP: Another question has arisen. What rolc does Jesus Christ play in this ongoing process of mankind and of the resurrection? Jesus himself was a historic person. He lived two thousand years ago. Millions of people lived before him, millions have lived after him. What is his role in the historic process of overcoming history and the boundaries between time and immortality?

BOULAD: Jesus Christ is the incarnation of the Logos. The Logos who is carrying the whole world in his spirit, in his inner being, has become flesh in Jesus Christ as St. John puts it, and has realised this event, taking over the process of evolution through his death and resurrection. I would say that Jesus' death and resurrection are the dramatisation or the historicity of a holistic drama of mankind in which the Logos is implied. And the Logos has become flesh in Jesus, so that we can understand that in dying he has occupied the centre of this sphere which we call mankind, and history, through the mystery of his life and resurrection. Through this central space, he is leading the process forward.

The Alpha, which is called Logos, and the Omega, which is also called Logos, is the same historical Jesus. Naturally, it cannot be proved, either mathematically or scientifically. It's also an act of faith, if you accept that the historical Jesus is the same at the beginning and the end. He is the new Adam, the totality of mankind, and he came to gather together, to collect together our different humanities. It is acceptable, it makes sense, but you can reject it if you wish. You are free to believe this Revelation. The act of faith is a free option. Some say that they would need more proof. They are free. It's a leap, a bet which you have to place. For me, Jesus Christ is the expression of the Logos incarnated, and the fulfillment of Adam. The second Adam makes a lot of sense through the writings of the New Testament, especially through St. Paul and St. John and the deep intuition expressed in their letters. I know that the link between the historical Jesus and the Pantocrator, the Omega point, is not always clear but needs to be developed further so that it is clear for mankind.

KAUP: You believe in Jesus as the catalyst for individual resurrection?

BOULAD: Yes, he is a catalyst who super-personalises each one of us in bringing him into touch with all the others. He is the soul of evolution, he is the spirit of evolution, he is the head of evolution. You can call it whatever you want but this is the idea. We need a focal point, not behind us but ahead of us, a focal point which is concentrating the whole in one. It's the eternal philosophical problem — the multiple and the one. From the very beginning of human thinking, you have this challenge — why is the world multiple, why is reality manifold when it should be one? It should be one in principle, but in reality it's multiple. Finding meaning does not mean finding it in your brain, it's realising it in history. I would express it like Marx who says that philosophers have thought history up until now, it's high time we shaped it.

I would say it is very good to think of immortality, to dream of the mystical body. It means having faith; it's philosophy, it gives meaning to my life, but this must be translated into commitment. I commit myself to building up this body, to realising immortality for all, through my life and through my love. This is the translation of faith into action, into engagement, otherwise it becomes hazy, abstract, theoretical, it remains a mere concept.

(Ref V)

Chapter 10:
A Personal Letter to Pope Benedict XVI - S.O.S. for Today's Church

By Rev. Henri Boulad, S.J.

Graz, Austria, 18th July 2007, later translated from the French by Richard Cross, New York and read by Fr. Boulad

This text, written in July 2007, was intended for the Pope only, as a private letter. An Austrian priest who had offered to hand it over to him thought after reading, that it would not be appropriate. He changed his mind.

Things remained that way, for two years until a friend of Fr Boulad in Canada, got the letter from him as a confidential document, in 2009. He started to spread it immediately through Internet. Given this situation, Fr Boulad thought it would be fair to send his letter to Pope Benedict by the official channel of the Nuncio in Cairo. This was done in September 2009, with a few words of apology. Till now, 2013, no answer from the Vatican. But this document, originally written in French, is now circulating in more languages : French, English, German, Hungarian and Spanish (different countries in Latin America).

Dear Holy Father,

I am addressing you directly because my heart bleeds at the sight of the abyss into which our Church is sinking today. Please excuse my frankness that is filial and dictated both by the "freedom of the children of God" to which St. Paul has called us as well as by my passionate love for the Church. Perhaps you will excuse the alarmist tone of this letter, for I believe that it is already the eleventh hour and that confronting the present situation must not be further delayed.

Introduction

Let me first of all present myself. I am an Egyptian-Lebanese Jesuit of the Melkite rite. Soon I will be 80 years old. For many years I have been the rector of the Jesuit College in Cairo after having served in the following capacities: superior of the Jesuits in Alexandria, regional superior of all the Jesuits in Egypt, professor of theology in Cairo, director of Caritas-Egypt, and vice-president of Caritas Internationalis for the Middle East and North Africa.

I know the Catholic hierarchy of Egypt quite well, having participated in its gatherings for several years in my role as President of the General Assembly of Religious Superiors in Egypt. I have very close personal relations with each of them - some of whom are my former students. Furthermore I personally know the Coptic Pope Chenouda III whom I frequently visit.

As for the Catholic hierarchy in Europe I have had many occasions to meet personally this one or that one of its members such as Cardinal Koenig, Cardinal Schoenborn, Cardinal Martini, Cardinal Daneels, Cardinal Sterzinsky, Archbishop Kothgasser, the diocesan Bishops Kapellari and Küng, other Austrian bishops, and bishops from other

European countries. These meetings took place during my participation at annual conferences in Austria, Germany, Switzerland, Hungary, France and Belgium. During these events I spoke to various groups as well as to the media (newspapers, radio and TV). I did the same in Egypt and the Middle East.

I have visited some fifty countries on four continents and have published over thirty works in fifteen languages, especially French, Arabic, Hungarian and German. Among my fifteen books in German you have once read and liked *Gottessöhne, Gottestöchter* that your friend Father Erich Fink from Bavaria gave you.

I do not say all of this out of vanity, Holy Father, but to tell you simply that my proposals are founded on a real knowledge of the universal Church and its situation today in 2007.

The Purpose of This Letter

I come now to the purpose of this letter in which I will try to be as brief, clear and objective as possible. First of all, a list of a certain number of realities — by no means exclusive.

1. Religious practice is in constant decline. The churches of Europe and Canada are only frequented by an increasing number of aging people who will soon be gone. There will be nothing left to do but close churches or transform them into museums, mosques, club houses or municipal libraries - something that is already under way. What surprises me is that many churches are already in the process of renovation and modernization at great expense in order to attract the faithful. But it is not such things that will stop the exodus.

2. Seminaries and novitiates are emptying at the same rate and vocations are in freefall. The future is rather sombre

and we must wonder who can take up the work. More and more European parishes are actually being taken up by Asian and African priests.

3. Many priests are leaving the priesthood. The small number of those who still continue their ministry and who are well past the retirement age have to serve multiple parishes in an expeditious and administrative manner. Many of them, both in Europe as well as in the Third World live in concubinage -in full view and knowledge of their parishioners who often approve them, and their bishop who can do nothing about it given the shortage of priests.

4. The language of the Church is out of date, anachronistic, boring, repetitious, and totally unsuited to our age. It is not at all a matter of going with the flow or of accommodation, because the message of the Gospel ought to be presented uncooked and to the point. What is needed rather is to move to that new "evangelization" to which John Paul II called us. Contrary to what many people think, it consists in not repeating toothless old stuff, but rather in innovating and inventing a new language that recasts the faith in a pertinent and meaningful way for men and women of today.

5. None of this can happen without an in-depth renewal of theology and catechesis that has to be rethought and reformulated from top to bottom. A priest and German religious I recently met told me that the word "mystical" was not mentioned once in the New Catechism. I was flabbergasted. It is clear that our faith is very cerebral, abstract and dogmatic. It speaks little to the heart or the body.

6. As a result, a great number of Christians are turning to the religions of Asia, to sects, to New Age, to evangelical churches, occultism and more. Why be surprised? They are seeking elsewhere the nourishment that they don't find with us, for they have the impression that we are giving them often

stones instead of bread. The Christian faith that once gave meaning to people's lives has become for them today an enigma, the leftovers of a dead past.

7. In the matter of morality and ethics, the injunctions of the Magisterium, repeated *ad nauseam* on marriage, divorce, contraception, abortion, homosexuality, clerical celibacy, divorce and remarriage, etc. touch nobody and only engender weariness and indifference. All these moral and pastoral problems deserve more than pre-emptory declarations. They deserve an approach that is a pastoral, sociological, psychological and humane approach in a way more in keeping with the Gospel.

8. The Catholic Church, which has been the great European educator for centuries, seems to have forgotten that this same Europe has grown up. Adult Europe today refuses to be treated like a child. The paternalistic style of a *Mater et Magistra* Church is definitely off the mark and no longer fits the bill today. Our Christian people have learned to think for themselves and are not about to swallow whatever comes along.

9. The nations once most Catholic — France, "the eldest daughter of the Church," or ultra-Catholic French Canada - have made a 180 degree turn toward atheism, anti-clericalism, agnosticism and indifference. For a number of other European countries the process is on-going. One notices that the more a people has been nurtured and mothered by the Church the greater is the reaction against her.

10. Dialogue with other Churches and religions is today in a disquieting decline. The remarkable advances realized over the past half century seem at this time compromised.

Faced with this rather overwhelming situation the Church's reaction is twofold.

- It tends to minimize the gravity of the reality and consoles itself by considering a certain renewal taking place in its most traditional wing as well as in the Third World.

- It invokes confidence in the Lord who has sustained the Church throughout twenty centuries and who will be able to help it overcome this new crisis as He has done in ages past. Doesn't the Church have His promises for eternal life?

My response to this

It is not by collecting shards under the buttresses of the past that one will resolve the problems of today and tomorrow. The apparent vitality of the Church in the Third World is deceptive. In all likelihood these new churches will sooner or later pass through the same crises as old Christian Europe.

The road to modernity cannot be by-passed and it is precisely because the Church has forgotten this that we have such a crisis today. Vatican II tried to make up for the four centuries it had lost, but today one has the impression that the Church is in the process of once more closing the doors that had been opened and is tempted to turn back to Trent and Vatican I rather than Vatican II. We should recall the injunction repeated several times by Pope John-Paul II: "there is no alternative to Vatican II."

How long are we going to engage in the politics of the ostrich and bury our heads in the sand? How long will we refuse to look things in the face? How long will we keep trying to salvage the façade at any price — a façade that deceives no one today? How long will we continue to cringe and take aim at any criticism rather than seeing in it a chance for renewal? How long are we going to put off till doomsday a reformation that is imperative and has been avoided far too long?

It is in resolutely looking to the future and not the past that the Church will accomplish her mission of being a "light to the world, salt of the earth, leaven to the dough." What we see today unfortunately is that the Church is dragging behind our times, after having led the world for centuries.

I must repeat what I said at the opening of this letter: It is the eleventh hour! *fünf vor zwölf!* History is not waiting, certainly not in our era when time is galloping at an ever rapid pace.

When people notice something wrong or dysfunctional in any commercial enterprise they immediately question what's happening, call in the experts, make corrections, and mobilize all their forces to address the crisis. Why can't the Church do the same thing? Why not mobilize all her living forces for a radical *aggiornamento?* Why? Could it be just sluggishness, cowardice, pride, lack of imagination and creativity, culpable passivity — all in the hope that the Lord will take care of things and that the Church well knows about such things, from its past?

Christ warned us in the Gospel: "The children of darkness are much more adept in managing their affairs than the children of light."

The Church today has an urgent and demanding need for the three-fold reform:

1. A Theological and Catechetical Reform to rethink the faith and reformulate it in a coherent manner for our contemporaries. A faith that no longer means anything, that does not give meaning to human existence, is simply an ornament, a useless superstructure that falls under its own weight. This is the case today.

2. A Pastoral Reform that rethinks from top to bottom the structures inherited from the past, (see my suggestions in this matter).

3. A Spiritual Reform to give new life to the mystical dimension, and a rethinking of the sacraments in view of giving them an existential dimension, and anchoring them to new life. I would have much to say on this. The Church of today is too formal, too formalistic. One has the impression that the institution stifles charisma and what ultimately counts is external stability, superficial respectability - a kind of facade. Don't we risk seeing ourselves one day treated as "whitened sepulchers" by Jesus?

Conclusion

To conclude, I suggest the calling together, at a universal level, of a general synod in which all Christians participate - Catholics and others - to examine, in all frankness and clarity, the points made here as well as all else that would be proposed. Such a synod, which would last three years, would culminate in a general assembly (let's avoid the term "council') that would bring together the results of this synod and draw some conclusions.

Finally, Most Holy Father, asking you to forgive my frankness and audacity and begging your paternal blessing. Allow me to say that I lived these days in your presence, thanks to your remarkable book, *Jesus of Nazareth (I)*, which is the object of my spiritual reading and daily meditation.

Sincerely yours in the Lord,

P. Henri Boulad, sj

ADDENDUM

Rethinking the Church's Pastoral Approach in Today's World

1. Restructuring the parish

Before being a Christian community, the parish, first of all, ought to be a human community; that is, an organic entity that exemplifies a certain number of social relationships as in a large family. This large family once was "the village" where everyone knew everyone else and where the pastor knew everyone personally, his or her past and present history. The pastor then lived the way Jesus described the Good Shepherd: "I know mine and mine know me."

This is possible in a grouping of a hundred people or at best a hundred families. Beyond such a number there is no longer community, but an anonymous group that defies unity and structure. The parish ceases to be a large family and the pastor can no longer be someone who "knows each one of this flock by name." He becomes an administrator who manages this gathering by the computer, by numbers and statistics with an Internet program. Or he concentrates on a small number of persons to the detriment of the rest.

Our country parishes of former days have changed in their dimension, becoming mega-churches with thousands of faithful. To insist on maintaining the present structure that is inherited from the past is an absurdity.

I believe a parish of a thousand inhabitants ought to be divided into a hundred mini parishes in order to become communities at a human level. I can already hear the objection: but where are you going to find a hundred priests to serve these new communities when we are having all the trouble in the world to recruit just one priest for the actual parishes? The reply is simple, so very simple.

2. Make an appeal to mature and proven men *(viri probati)* to take over these individual communities and give resident pastors the title of bishop of this new ensemble of parishes. In each group of homes or neighbourhood the Church would single out a serious Christian, having proven himself- preferably a retired person in good health, with a decent pension and sufficient leisure time for him to assume the pastoral charge of his community, in these days when we see that people are living longer and retire earlier it would not be hard to find such a person. His human, theological and spiritual formation would be completed through intensive courses for a period of six months. This would also be a period of probation. Once completed, the person would be ordained.

Having accepted such a proposition, he would obviously consult with his wife who in turn would become his right arm and indispensable collaborator in running the parish. And the role of this pastor would consist in getting to know each of the families and each individual personally. This is done by home visitation, celebrating anniversaries, different get-togethers, meetings for reflection and all this through his own initiative and the suggestions of his parishioners.

There would be Eucharistic celebrations also in the homes as needed, and on Sundays people would gather in a large hall for Mass followed by an agape of refreshments.

This priest would be responsible for everyone in his parish - believers and non-believers. Without imposing anything it would be up to him to find the right formula to put everyone at ease. Thus there would be parishes of variable size. This is a challenge that would demand of the pastor tact, a right approach, discretion, flexibility and creativity

Given such a perspective,

3. Married men would be ordained, just as is the case in the Eastern Churches, Orthodox and Catholic Uniate, and as has been the case for centuries in the rest of Christianity. The practice of celibacy has always been reserved to individuals - monks and religious - who freely chose this lifestyle that supposes a supportive community. It is from these that one would choose the bishops but to impose celibacy on all priests without distinction under the pretext that this constitutes for some a valuable and viable path is tempting God. The consequence of this is that there are an impressive number of Roman Catholic priests living in concubinage both in Europe and on all continents.

Is it not unreasonable to demand that a man, who does not have the calling to celibacy, lives year after year in isolation, alone within the walls of his rectory? Didn't God Himself say in the opening pages of the Bible "It is not good for man to live alone?"

The stubbornness of the Western Catholic Church in this matter is beyond explanation and is in contradiction with the ancient tradition of the Church. It is about time that the Magisterium of the Roman Catholic Church stops its fidgeting and opens the door to a married priesthood in consort with an optional celibate priesthood, given the perspective of this pastoral reorganization that I propose,

4. A vocation would be less a calling by God than a direct call by the Church to an individual.

A person would be completely free to accept or refuse this call. Having said this, one must not exclude a direct call; from God to the soul.

A final point:

5. Aside from the geographic parishes I have described, one would also envision parishes that are socially selective; that do not depend so much on where one lives as on one's profession or sphere of interests. Such parishes would be created according to the needs and function of the existing groups of people. The idea here is to start with a group that is already established and help it pass from a naturally human community to a Christian community. The Christian element should not be superimposed on the already existing community but act as a leaven in the dough to animate it from within.

In conclusion, I would say that the Spirit today calls us to reflect, to invent and innovate: to come out of our preconceived notions and our set categories; to risk a new pastoral approach that responds to the needs of our day. No more timidity, no more caution, no more hesitation. "Fear not" said John-Paul II; "Fear not" says the Lord throughout the Bible. We must once again find the creativity and boldness of Saint Paul. Will we remain prisoners of the past forever? Will we know how to invent the future? ***(Ref W)***

Chapter 11
Who is Henri Boulad?

It is appropriate to conclude this book of extracts from Fr Boulad's writings by including the introductory chapter to his latest book on Reconciliation, *He who forgives is like God.* This chapter has been written by Hidda Westenberger, who has also helped a great deal in the assembling of this book of extracts.

"When you shoot an arrow of truth, dip its point in honey" - an Arab proverb

The Egyptian Jesuit father Henri Boulad, is a mystic fired by the Holy Spirit and at the same time an intellectual thinker who was trained in the West, a guilty past he claims can be redeemed. Genuine repentance and acts of forgiveness are not just part of a psychological debate but a spiritual process on a higher level and consequently an essential aspect of our own individual resurrection. "Today" Paradise is promised to the thief on the cross near Jesus and not some time in the future. This means a close living union in Christ - "with me" Jesus pointed out. Can spiritually guilty actions be blotted out? This is comforting to whoever understands it and can accept it. This latest book explains various aspects and examples of Father Boulad's vision: it is founded on an unshakeable spiritual joy, in our present world as well as transcending space and time. To a certain extent this mission has already been accomplished, when man will be perfect and "God will be all in all".

The nature of forgiveness concerns each one of us, actively or passively, with no exception, as a result of injuries and incriminations, remorse and self-accusations, or even fear of hell, or part of the unconditional love which we receive or give. A book with this title by this popular author who has already written 14 books –all published in Austria- is a plea for the perfection of Divine Love and no one can escape. His readers have known for years that what he says, based on his own personal experience, is presented in an authentic and enthusiastic approach. Henri Boulad conveys the certainty of Salvation. What more would our Christian world need today? He is a "true prophet for our time".

Fr Boulad is an Arab Christian of Syrian and Lebanese origin, born in Alexandria in 1931 where he still lives today. He is a Greek-Catholic , therefore in union with Rome, and his rite is Byzantine. He celebrates Mass in three different rites: Coptic Catholic, Greek Catholic and Roman Catholic. When he tours Europe where he gives sought-after lectures and says mass, he sometimes unexpectedly starts chanting an Arab song which sounds out of place, or else he dismisses the congregation with a Coptic blessing.

He comes from a real Eastern family but his mother tongue and culture are clearly French. This explains why, while not in possession of a French passport, he has been decorated by the French -*Ordre National du Mérite* and *Ordre des Palmes Académiques*. His books, which I compile using his lecture scripts and translate into German, deliberately contain some French words –with translation- in order to leave the personal touch.

At the age of 16 Henri Boulad experienced his Damascus moment, and this was the start of his vocation! This was so obviously clear to him that he still remembers the exact time when it happened, at 3 pm on the flat roof of his father's house in Alexandria. From then on the course of his life changed radically. He jettisoned all his dreams and cast aside his artistic talent. He wanted to devote all his future life to "the total surrender of himself for the happiness of men and God". And to this day he gives of himself unreservedly. His spiritual energy and his love of his neighbour never falter; a love experienced by all those who come close him. The word "holiday" is not yet part of his vocabulary.

I can vouch for everything I say here, as I have known him for more than 30 years, several of which were spent in Egypt where my husband worked for the World Health Organisation. Years later the director of a spiritual formation center in Salzburg joked on introducing Father Boulad before the lecture, "Madame Westenberger discovered him in the Egyptian desert and she brought him over to us." Not long after I started finding out about him in Alexandria, my friend there whispered these words which I have never forgotten, "We must now spread his sphere of influence, he should be speaking on European television every day, this would solve many problems." At least today there are books available and lecture tours around Europe.

His talks are inspired by his life, everything he says is rooted in his experience. Thanks also to the legendary and never-ending Jesuit training (14 years which he endured, albeit feeling somewhat restless but always showing submission in Beirut, Paris and Chicago. His subjects were wonderful ones: Theology, Psychology, Philosophy, Mysticism and Literature). As members of his Order never stay put, he was given varied responsibilities, for instance as Head of Caritas Egypt for 12 years, 5 of which spent as Vice-President of Caritas International. The impact of those years on him was crucial! This explains why in this book we find him re-iterating his warning against "the contagious social sin" which is becoming more and more dire all over the world. This is why he regards it as the original sin. He encourages all those who have any sense to change course before it is too late. For many years he was also Head of three Jesuit Colleges in Cairo, with 1600 students, 60 per cent of whom were Muslims- and the parents were not amongst the easiest to deal with.

Typical of him is his way of travelling with his bag and his flight ticket, between Canada, Europe and the Arab world, organising retreats and lecturing. He likes and admires Europeans and their undertakings. He understands human beings, he understands our world and he is familiar with Islam. He lives in close union with God, and understands our mission in the world. Every time he meets people, they experience truth, honesty and a radical approach on his part. I would go as far as to say that he speaks with the serene cheerfulness characteristic of some saints. Others have had the same impression.

The book is illustrated: it contains a plethora of passages drawn from life full of energy and colour. Being Eastern Fr Boulad is a born story-teller. Many times he deals with love, the enemy of evil! Love forgives, operates on the spiritual level. It knows how to sacrifice and make the person like God. Yet, there is one thing this book is not, and that is material for theologians. It is with great optimism that one puts it in the hands of those searching for spiritual answers, people who are feeling lost. In its German version the text remains easily accessible, as it does in the French original, thus reflecting the way he speaks freely in front of a microphone, always keeping eye contact with his audience, remaining tangible, existential, and charismatic.

Human beings are what he cherishes most, and the way they mature towards resurrection. In God's hand the individual is protected and is prepared for eternity. He needs our help in acts of forgiveness between human beings. Repentance and reconciliation are part of the purification process on our common route to fulfilment. Henri Boulad recognizes the mystical and fiery core of resurrection in each one of us.

In this study of forgiveness Fr Boulad presents several levels: the secret, intimate level where guilt and quiet repentance dwell; the painful level of our personal relationships – love and marriage, eros and agape, work with the young; the heroic level, love of one's enemies which has a pacifying influence from the private sphere to the political one; the difficult level, the official Church asking for forgiveness as initiated by Pope John-Paul II, or the new ecumenical approach; finally the sacramental level of the traditional confession, but also confession under the label of "universal priesthood" (last Council) that is between believers which is no less effective.

Where does this priest stand? Is he progressive and liberal or traditional? It is best not to pigeon-hole him as he hates labels for himself as well as for others and doesn't allow himself be categorised. Henri Boulad is humble. He builds bridges. He is not a revolutionary and he doesn't want clashes between traditional and modern approaches. Instead he seeks to unite and strengthen people's positions because each is acquainted with an aspect of the truth. This is why his present Superior, the Provincial in Lebanon, has asked him to compile a synthesis of faith in our time – in accordance with the new evangelization as recommended by Pope John-Paul II. He has been making this appeal for decades now. He knows only too well that we must strive to find new approaches and a new language for this evangelization; in part one must go beyond the decisions made during the last Council! So in this book we can find pointers towards a more widespread use of the sacraments. Fr Boulad has been searching and he encourages us also to do the same. A remark of his which is familiar to us, "I would like to add an eleventh commandment to the Decalogue – thou shalt seek".

(Ref Y)

THE ELEVENTH COMMANDMENT: YOU SHALL SEARCH! YOU SHALL CREATE

O God,
you have created me for something great
and you have given me the responsibility
for my own life,
to achieve it to its full capacity.
Lord,
don't let me live my life to the half or in a tedious way.
I would like to glorify you
by placing my whole being in a state of growing,
of outgrowing,
day after day, moment after moment.
Help me to develop and to maximise
all the potential, all the talents you have given me,
all the richness hidden within myself.
I have no right, oh God,
to hide the talents you gave me under the ground,
but I must develop them for the benefit of mankind,
and feel my responsibility toward history
by making things better and changing them for the best.
Don't let me be a spectator to what happens,
but an actor, an agent.
Let me feel that you count on me,
that you will not do things that I can do.

(Ref J)

The only book in English by Father Henri Boulad s.j.

All is Grace, Man and the Mystery of Time

Books by Father Kenneth Payne:

Stretch Out Your Hand
(Instruction in the faith for Non-Catholics)

Shades of Welcome
(The importance of openness and welcoming in our lives)

What Shall I Say?
Columba Press
(Homily Suggestions for the three year cycle)

Central Line to Eziat
(Thought provoking fiction, including travel and providence)

Thoughts, Anecdotes and Stories from a Priest's Notebook
(Amusing and revelatory)

Joy for All?
(The story of Father Richard Ho Lung, founder of the Missionaries of the Poor)

The Rosary for Today
McCrimmon Press
(New ways of saying the Rosary)

Questions Children Ask, With Possible Answers
McCrimmon Press
(Useful for parents, teachers and even grandparents!)

* 9 7 8 1 7 8 0 3 5 7 4 8 5 *

ND - #0183 - 060826 - C0 - 210/148/13 - PB - 9781780357485 - Gloss Lamination